mine

by **Polly Teale**

SHARED EXPERIENCE

Shared Experience is committed to creating theatre
that goes beyond our everyday lives, giving form
to the hidden world of emotion and imagination.

We see the rehearsal process as a genuinely open
forum for asking questions and taking risks that define
the possibilities of performance.

At the heart of the company's work is the power and
excitement of the performer's physical presence
and the collaboration between actor and audience
– a shared experience.

Lorraine Stanley, Katy Stephens & Sophie Stone

'Shared Experience is one of the most distinctive theatre companies in the land. Those who have seen the company are unlikely to forget its thrilling productions'

'Shared Experience are in a league of their own' Time Out

Shared Experience has been instrumental in pioneering a distinctive performance style that celebrates the union of physical and text-based theatre. Consistently dedicated to innovation and exploration, the company enjoys outstanding artistic and critical success at home and abroad.

Shared Experience has toured extensively, from Buenos Aires to Beijing, from New York to Delhi. The company's work ranges from adaptations of novels to contemporary and classic drama.

"I'd spend hours rearranging the furniture. It was my favourite place in all the world. Used to dream about it. Dream I was living inside it. Like it had grown or I'd shrunk and it was real. Like it had come to life and everything was just exactly as it was in the dolls house. Like the food was stuck on the plates and the drawers wouldn't open and the flowers in the wallpaper were huge. And the others, the others were dolls. I'm the only one who's real and… I want to go downstairs. I want to get out but I remember, I realise that there are no stairs. You can't get down. Get out."

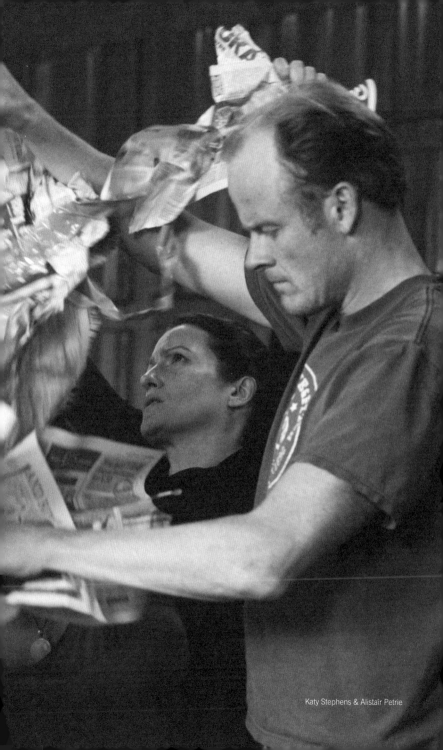

Katy Stephens & Alistair Petrie

"Do you remember how we used to spend all day in the river in the woods. We weren't allowed to get out. Like the land was another country that we'd never go back to. We'd lose track of time. Forget to go home until it was dark. All day with our feet in the water. Picking our way through the stones and the weeds and the roots of trees. And all day the sound. The sound of the river in our ears. Let's not go back. Let's never go back to the house. Let's live out here. Sleep out here under the trees. Climb up into the branches if anyone tries to get us. Let's never go home again."

Sophie Stone

Marion Bailey

Katy Stephens

"I undress her. Look at her body. Try to remember. To learn it by heart. Everything. Every detail so's when she's gone I'll be able to imagine. Imagine I'm holding her. Feel her weight. Her smell. See her weird little toes. The soft hair on her back. Like a monkey. The birthmark on her cheek. Then I think maybe I shouldn't, in case I miss her too much and I can't stand it and I wish I never saw her. Never smelt, felt, touched. But it's too late now. I done it haven't I. Let her in. Let her in to me."

Clare Lawrence Moody & Lorraine Stanley

mine

by **Polly Teale**

THE COMPANY

Marion Bailey	Mother
Clare Lawrence Moody	Sister/Katya
Alistair Petrie	Man
Lorraine Stanley	Rose
Katy Stephens	Woman
Sophie Stone	Child

Other parts played by members of the company

Director	**Polly Teale**
Designer	**Angela Simpson**
Music & Sound	**Peter Salem**
Company Movement	**Liz Ranken**
Lighting	**Colin Grenfell**
Video & Projection Design	**Thomas Gray for The Gray Circle**
Sound Design	**Alex Caplen**
Dramaturg	**Nancy Meckler**
Production Manager	**Alison Ritchie**
Company Stage Manager	**Chrissie Chandler**
Deputy Stage Manager	**Sarah Tryfan**
Costume Supervisor	**Yvonne Milnes**
Props	**Simon Hodgson**
Tour Relights	**Will Evans**
Sound Engineer	**Owen Lasch**
Wardrobe	**Naomi Weight**
Assistant Director	**Anna Ehnold-Danailov**
Casting	**Sam Jones**
Dialect	**Jan Haydn Rowles**
Marketing	**Mark Slaughter for makesthree marketing & promotion**
Press	**Clióna Roberts**
Education Pack	**Bailey Lock**

Scenery contracted & painted by **Bowerwood**, backcloth painted by **Chris Clark** and projection equipment supplied by **XL Video**.

The performance will last approximately 2hrs 15 mins including one interval.

COMPANY

Back row from left: Simon Hodgson, Sarah Tryfan, Thomas Gray, Anna Ehnold-Danailov, Alistair Petrie, Tristan Bernays, Harriet Balsom, Colin Grenfell, Yvonne Milnes.
Second row from left: Bailey Lock, Alison Ritchie, Liz Ranken, Polly Teale, Lorraine Stanley, Chrissie Chandler, Sharon John, Angela Simpson. **Front row from left:** Jon Harris, Katy Stephens, Sam Jones, Sophie Stone, Clare Lawrence Moody, Marion Bailey.

Marion Bailey

Mother

Theatre includes: For Shared Experience: *War and Peace, Kindertransport.* Other credits include: *The Arab-Israeli Cookbook, Dance of Death* (Tricycle); *Incomplete and Random Acts of Kindness, Blessed Be the Tie, This is a Chair, Hush, Beside Herself, Panic, Falkland Sound* (Royal Court); *Holes in the Skin* (Chichester Festival Theatre); *Normal, All of You Mine* (Bush); *Cloud Nine* (Old Vic); *A Delicate Balance* (Nottingham Playhouse); *Man Beast and Virtue, Black Snow* (RNT); *Bad Blood* (Gate); *Loving Women* (Arts Theatre); *Where There is Darkness, Favourite Nights* (Lyric); *Raspberry* (Soho Theatre/Edinburgh Festival); *Lazy Days Limited* (Stratford East); *Goose-Pimples* (Hampstead Theatre/West End).

Television includes: *Midsomer Murders, Monday Monday, Persuasion, Holby City, New Tricks, The Bill, Derailed, The Thing About Vince, Under the Sun, Dalziel and Pascoe, Harvey Moon, Casualty, Dangerfield, A Touch of Frost, Inspector Morse, Poirot, Stay Lucky, To Have and To Hold, Charlie, Big Deal, Jury, Raspberry.*

Film includes: *Vera Drake, I'll Be There, All or Nothing, Nasty Neighbours, Way Upstream, Solzhenitsyn, Meantime.*

Clare Lawrence Moody

Sister/Katya

Theatre includes: *Fram* (RNT); *Night School, Whale Music* (Kings Head); *Three Sisters* (Tron Theatre/Theatre Royal Haymarket Gala); *Strip Show* (EdFringe/ Kings Head); *The Alchemist, The Changeling* (Cambridge Playroom).

As co-founder of Out Of The Blue Ltd, theatre productions include: *This Is Our Youth, Oleanna* (Garrick); *A Life in The Theatre, Fool For Love* (Apollo); *Some Girls* (Gielgud); *Five Kinds of Silence* (Lyric Hammersmith).

Television includes: *Eastenders, Ultimate Force, Bad Girls III, Longitude, This Could Be The Last Time, Harry, The Bill.*

Alistair Petrie

Man

Theatre includes: *His Dark Materials, Henry IV pts 1 & 2, Playing With Fire* (RNT); *Pravda* (Chichester/Birmingham Rep); *Excuses* (Soho Theatre); *Troilus and Cressida* (RSC); *Brand* (RSC/Theatre Royal Haymarket); *The Importance Of Being Earnest* (Australia/ Savoy); *Herakles* (Gate); *Charley's Aunt* (Norwich Playhouse); *The Grapes of Wrath, A Midsummer Night's Dream* (Northcott); *Great Expectations* (Theatre Clwyd/Tour).

Television includes: *Cranford, Mutual Friends, The Whistleblowers, Flood, The Forsyte Saga, Second Sight, The Stretch, Dalziel and Pascoe, McCorquodale's Barnet, The Soviets, Jonathan Creek, Game On, Emma, Murder in the Family, All Quiet on the Preston Front, Demob, Scarlet and Black.*

Film includes: *The Duchess, The Bank Job, The Mark of Cain, A Bunch of Amateurs, Mrs Dalloway, Man to Man, Car Stories.*

Katy Stephens

Woman

Theatre includes: *The Histories* (RSC);
Tamburlaine (Bristol Old Vic/Barbican);
*The Seagull, Ion, Macbeth, The White
Devil, The Three Sisters, The Europeans,
The Caucasian Chalk Circle, Blood
Wedding, The Recruiting Officer* (Mercury
Theatre); *Twelfth Night, Sleeping Beauty,
Our Day Out, Silas Marner* (Belgrade
Theatre); *David Copperfield, I Don't Want
To Set The World On Fire* (New Victoria,
Newcastle); *A Midsummer Night's
Dream* (Orchard Theatre Co).

Television includes: *The Bill, London's
Burning, Ellington, Fun Song Factory, Wow.*

Film includes: *Relative Values.*

Lorraine Stanley

Rose

Theatre includes: *Frontline* (Globe); *Days
of Significance* (RSC); *Look at Me* (London/
Tour); *Gina in Care* (Haringey Theatre);
Widowers' Houses (RNT/Tour); *To Kill
A Mockingbird* (Mercury Theatre).

Television includes: *The Bill, Little Dorrit,
He Kills Coppers, Trial and Retribution,
Waking the Dead, Vivien Vile, Inspector
Linley, Casualty, Eastenders, Making Waves,
Rehab, London's Burning, Anybody's
Nightmare, Nicholas Nickleby, Spooks.*

Film includes: *Cass, Eden Lake, London
to Brighton, Royalty, Gangster No 1.*

Sophie Stone

Child

Trained: RADA

Theatre includes: *Multiplex, Fen, You Make
Me Happy (When Skies are Grey), Flying*
(The Watermill).

Theatre at RADA includes: *Vinegar Tom,
The Importance of Being Earnest, A Servant
to Two Masters, Women Beware Women,
The Fair Penitent, Gulliver's Travels, Look
Back In Anger, Little Eyolf, Dolly West's
Kitchen, Man Equals Man, Prairie Du Chien.*

Television includes: *Casualty.*
Television at RADA: *Breaking Up.*

CREATIVE TEAM

Polly Teale

Polly Teale
Director

Polly is Joint Artistic Director of Shared Experience. For Shared Experience: *Ten Tiny Toes, Kindertransport, Jane Eyre* (adapted and directed), *Brontë, After Mrs Rochester* (written and directed – Best Director, Evening Standard Awards; Best West End Production, Time Out Awards), *Madame Bovary, The Clearing, A Doll's House, The House of Bernarda Alba, Desire Under the Elms.* Co-directed with Nancy Meckler: *War and Peace* and *Mill on the Floss.*

Other theatre includes: *Angels and Saints* (Soho Theatre); *The Glass Menagerie* (Lyceum, Edinburgh); *Miss Julie* (Young Vic); *Babies, Uganda, Catch* (Royal Court); *A Taste of Honey* (ETT); *Somewhere* (RNT); *Waiting at the Water's Edge* (Bush); *What Is Seized* (Drill Hall).

Other writing includes: *Afters* (BBC Screen Two); *Fallen* (Traverse, Edinburgh/Drill Hall).

Angela Simpson
Designer

Angela studied Fine Art at Middlesex University before completing the Motley Theatre Design Course.

Design credits include: For Shared Experience: *Ten Tiny Toes.* As Set Designer: *War and Peace.* As Associate Set Designer: *Jane Eyre.* Other credits include: *A Conversation* (Royal Exchange); *The Doll Tower* (LLT/Unity Theatre); *Darwin's Dream* (Royal Albert Hall); *The Baby and Fly Pie, Basil & Beattie, Habitat* (Royal Exchange Studio); *Map of the Heart* (Salisbury Playhouse); *The Pocket Dream, The Derby McQueen Affair* (York Theatre Royal); *Under the Curse, Habitats* (Gate); *Unsung/ Consuming Songs* (BAC); *The Danny Crowe Show* (Dundee Rep); *Kom_b@* (RNT Studio); *L'Enfant et les Sortileges, L'Heure Espanol* (RSAMD); *Crime and Punishment in Dalston* (Arcola); *Bread and Butter* (Southwark Playhouse); *Change of Heart* (New End Theatre); *Comedy of Errors* (Oval House); *A Midsummer Night's Dream, Extension Treble Zero, Anansi, Boubile* (Chicken Shed); *Royalty* (So Loose Films). Angela has also exhibited her sculpture in galleries in London.

Peter Salem
Music & Sound

For Shared Experience: *Ten Tiny Toes, War and Peace, Kindertransport, Orestes, Brontë, A Passage to India, The Clearing, Mill on the Floss, The House of Bernarda Alba, Jane Eyre, The Tempest, Anna Karenina.*

Other theatre credits include: *The Crucible, The Miser*, Robert Lépage's *A Midsummer Night's Dream* (RNT); *Julius Caesar, Murder in the Cathedral* (RSC); and work for the Royal Court, Traverse, Lyric Hammersmith and Nottingham Playhouse. Peter's contemporary dance scores have been performed by Second Stride and Zaragosa Ballet Company.

Film and TV credits include: *Sex, the City and Me*, *Beau Brummell*, *Falling*, *Trial and Retribution*, *Thursday the 12th*, *Great Expectations*, *Alive and Kicking*, *The Vice*, *Painted Lady*, *Venice*, *The Power of Art: Caravaggio*, *Thrown to the Lions*, *Sea of Cortez*, *21Up*, *The Spy Who Caught a Cold*, *I Met Adolf Eichmann*, *Eight Hours From Paris*, *Three Salons at the Seaside*, *What Makes Me Happy*.

Liz Ranken

Liz Ranken
Movement Director

For Shared Experience: *Ten Tiny Toes*, *War and Peace*, *Kindertransport*, *Orestes*, *Madame Bovary*, *A Passage to India*, *A Doll's House*, *Jane Eyre*, *The House of Bernarda Alba*, *The Tempest*, *Mill on the Floss*, *Anna Karenina*. As Director and Performer: *Summat A-do-wi Weddins* (Place Portfolio Choreographic Award);

Theory of Love; *Ooh*; *Funk Off Green* (Capital Award); *Venus and Adonis* (with Rebecca McCutcheon). As Performer: *Terminatress* (with Rae Smith); *The Big Tease* (Grassmarket Project); work with Gloria, CAT A Company ENO. Founder member of DV8. Winner of the 1992 Dance Umbrella Time Out Award.

Liz is an Associate Movement Director for the RSC and completed the Henry Cycle in 2007. She has also worked extensively with Dominic Cooke including *Arabian Nights*, *Fireface* and *My Mother Said I Never Should*.

TV and film include: As Performer: *Silences*, *3 Steps to Heaven*, *Touched*, *Edward II*, *Pet Shop Boys Tour*. As Choreographer: *Alive and Kicking*. Liz also works professionally as a commissioned painter and has recently written a play: *Venus after Adonis*.

Colin Grenfell
Lighting Designer

Recent theatre credits include: *365*, *The Bacchae*, *Black Watch* (National Theatre of Scotland); *Single Spies* (Theatre Royal Bath); *Alex* (Arts Theatre); *Theatre of Blood*, *Spirit*, *The Hanging Man*, *Lifegame*, *Coma*, *Animo*, *70 Hill Lane* (Improbable); *Kes*, *Separate Tables* (Manchester Royal Exchange); *Touched* (Salisbury Playhouse); *Enjoy* (Watford Palace Theatre); *Unprotected* (Liverpool Everyman); *Casanova*, *Playing the Victim* (Told by an Idiot).

Opera credits include: extensive work for Opera Holland Park; *Fidelio* (Opera Touring Company Dublin); *La Bohème* (English Touring Opera).

Thomas Gray for The Gray Circle

Video & Projection Design

Theatre credits include: *The Lord of the Rings* (Theatre Royal, Drury Lane); *Dirty Dancing* (Hamburg); *3 Musketiere: Das Musical* (Stuttgart); *Memory Puzzle* (Taiwan); *Cinderella* (Goteborg Opera); *Testing the Echo* (Out of Joint); *Unprotected* (Liverpool Everyman); *Vernon God Little* (Young Vic); *Twilight of the Gods* (ENO); *His Dark Materials* (RNT); Ernest Bloch's *Macbeth* (Klang Bogen Wien); *ES* (Dance Theatre, LUDENS Tokyo); *Bound to Please, Happiest Day of my Life* (DV8, World Tours). Other projects include a 300 degree circular video screen for LG Electronics Las Vegas, video projections for Samsung's Olympic Pavilion, Diesel Jeans for London Fashion Week and Saatchi & Saatchi Advertising.

The Gray Circle is a London-based Moving Image and Installation Art company established by Thomas Gray in 1995. www.thegraycircle.com

Alex Caplen

Sound Designer

Alex began his career in theatrical sound at the Nuffield Theatre. Here he started as a sound operator and eventually moved on to design. For Shared Experience, Sound Design credits include: *Ten Tiny Toes*. As Assistant Sound Designer: *War and Peace*. As Sound Operator: *Kindertransport*. Other Sound Design credits include: *Peter Pan, Holes, Duck Variations* (Tour), *The Wizard of Oz* (Nuffield Theatre); *Imogen* (Oval House/Tour).

Sound Operator credits include: *Blood Brothers* (International Tour); *Ballroom* (Tour). Alex is a member of the Sound department at the Royal Court where his credits include: *The Pain and the Itch,* *Rhinoceros, The Arsonists, Free Outgoing, Now or Later, Gone too Far* (Hackney Empire).

Alex has also worked as a touring Front of House engineer for large scale music touring.

Alison Ritchie

Production Manager

Alison has worked on all Shared Experience's productions since *Heartbreak House* in 1989. She is also Production Manager for Grange Park Opera and does freelance contracts for the Royal Opera House and the University of the Arts, amongst others.

She is a trustee of Chicken Shed Theatre Company and a Board Member for Artsadmin.

Chrissie Chandler

Company Stage Manager

Chrissie graduated from the Welsh College of Music and Drama in 2001 with a BA Hons in Stage Management and Theatre Studies.

Credits include: *The Magic Flute, Il Trovatore, La Bohème, Chorus!, Parsifal, Le Nozze Di Figaro, The Elixir of Love, Don Giovanni, Cav & Pag, Die Fledermaus, Tosca, Madama Butterfly, Così Fan Tutte, Rigoletto, Cunning Little Vixen, Salome, La Clemenza de Tito, Leonore* (Welsh National Opera); *Happy Days, The Rose Tattoo* (RNT); *La Fanciulla Del West, The Magic Flute* (Grange Park Opera); *The Rake's Progress* (Royal College of Music); *What a Feeling* (Flying Music UK Tour); *A Chorus of Disapproval, Night Must Fall, The Druids Rest, Brassed Off* (Clywd Theatr Cymru Tour); *The Wizard of Oz* (Wales Millennium Centre); *Santa's Missing Trousers* (Torch Theatre); *Aladdin* (Corn Exchange, Newbury).

Sarah Tryfan
Deputy Stage Manager

Sarah graduated from RADA in 2001 with a diploma in Stage Management.

Recent Stage Management credits include: *The Ugly One*, *Birth of a Nation*, *The Arsonists*, *Scenes from the Back of Beyond* (Royal Court); *I'll Be The Devil* (RSC); *Falstaff*, *The Elixir of Love* (Grange Park Opera); *King of Hearts* (Out of Joint/ Hampstead Theatre).

Yvonne Milnes
Wardrobe Supervisor

Costume Design credits: For Shared Experience: *War and Peace*. Other credits include: *She Stoops To Conquer*, *Playboy Of The Western World* (Century Theatre, Keswick); *One Careful Owner* (Queen's Theatre, Hornchurch); *One Flew Over The Cuckoo's Nest*, *Canterbury Tales* (West End); *The Three Musketeers*, *Dracula*, *The Gift*, *Last Of The Mohicans*, *Frankenstein*, *A Tale Of Two Cities* (New Vic Theatre); *Doctor Who* (Mark Furness Productions); *Blackworks* (ICA); *Limelight*, *The Salisbury Proverbs* (Station House Opera); *Die Fledermaus* (Arts); *La Bohème*, *Eugene Onegin* (Music Theatre London); *Marvin's Room* (Hampstead Theatre/West End); *Watch My Lips* (Drill Hall); *South Pacific* (Grange Park Opera). As Associate Costume Designer: *Henry IV parts 1 and 2* (Washington Shakespeare Theatre Co).

Costume Supervisor credits include work for the following companies: Shared Experience, Garsington Opera, Royal Opera House, Shakespeare's Globe, Hampstead Theatre, Grange Park Opera, RNT, RSC, New National Theatre Tokyo, K Ballet Tokyo, Metropolitan Opera New York, Chichester Festival Theatre, San Francisco Ballet.

Simon Hodgson
Prop Maker

Trained: Motley Theatre Design Course.

As Assistant to the Designer credits include: For Shared Experience: *War and Peace*, *Ten Tiny Toes*. Other credits include: *The Vortex* (Apollo); *Priscilla: Queen of the Desert* (Palace Theatre); *Relatively Speaking* (Bath Theatre Royal); *Flashdance: the Musical* (UK Tour); *Doctor Dolittle* (UK Tour); *Six Characters in Search of an Author* (Traverse). Design credits include: *Prairie du Chein/Lakeboat* (RADA); *Pinter's People* (Theatre Royal Haymarket); *The Tempest* (Oval House); *The Pied Piper* (Wellingborough Castle).

Owen Lasch
Sound Operator

Trained: Degree in Sonic Art, Middlesex University

Film Sound Design credits include: *Loner*, *Hush*, *The Devine Seizure*, *One Day at a Time*, *Yarn*. Location Recording credits include: *Shish*, *Freedom Dance*. Sound Installations include: *Hoov Orkester*, *How Can I Be An Environmentalist When I Make Electronic Music* (Tress Untitled), *The Sonic Landscape*, *Found Sound Bus Journey Recreation* (Truman Brewery, London); *Title*, *Collaboration* (5pm Gallery). Music projects include: *Hills Are Mountains*, *W Von*, *Recording Artist Cleo*, *Oliekridt*, *Sal Sohwen*.

Will Evans

Tour Relights

Trained: Central School of Speech and Drama.

For Shared Experience: *War and Peace, Kindertransport, Orestes, Jane Eyre.* Other relights credits include: *Cassanova* (WYP/Told by an Idiot); *A Fine Balance* (Tamasha); *Street Trilogy* (Theatre Absolute); *HMS Pinafore* (Carl Rosa Opera); *Golden Boy* (Broadway Productions); *Something Else, The Snow Dragon* (Tall Stories/ Soho Theatre).

Lighting design credits include: *How did the Giraffe get its Neck?, Monster Hits, Does a Monster Live Next Door?, Cat and No Mouse* (Tall Stories); *Russian National Mail* (Sputnik Theatre, Teatr.doc – Moscow) *The Tempest* (Theatre Royal, Winchester); *Lady Chatterley's Lover* (Buxton Opera House/ Tour); *Honeymoon in Flames* (Greenhorn/ Paupers Pit); *Serenading Louie* (Aorta/GBS Theatre, RADA); *Legend of Perseus, Don't Let the Pigeon Drive the Bus!, The Night Before Christmas, Don't Let the Pigeon Stay Up Late!* (Big Wooden Horse Theatre/Tour); *Spend Spend Spend, 7 Lears* (Birmingham School of Acting).

Will is also on the executive of the Association of Lighting Designers.

Naomi Weight

Wardrobe Mistress

Naomi has a degree in textile science from Leeds University and a City & Guilds in Pattern Cutting, specialising in Corsetry.

Wardrobe Mistress credits include: For Shared Experience: *War and Peace.* Other credits include: Seasons for Garsington Opera; *The Wizard of Oz* (Royal Festival Hall); *Beauty and the Beast* (UK productions); *Snow White* (QDos Entertainment); *Las Vegas Fantasy 2* (Showstoppers Worldwide Entertainment/ Taiwan); and over three years on the Disney Cruise Line.

As Wardrobe Assistant: *Jack and the Beanstalk, Dick Whittington, Sweeney Todd* (York Theatre Royal); *Pinocchio* (Italy); *Cirque Surreal* (Edinburgh Festival); *Romeo & Juliet* (Northern Ballet Theatre); *Talking Heads, Don Quixote, American Buffalo* (Duke's Playhouse, Leeds); and has renovated costumes for Jorvik Viking Museum.

Anna Ehnold-Danailov

Assistant Director

Anna recently completed her Masters Degree in Directing at Central School of Speech and Drama, following her BA (Hons) at Central Saint Martins in Theatre Design.

As Director credits include: *STILL* (International Workshop Festival, London); *Metamorphosis, Better Morphosis* (Cochrane Theatre); *Flora* (Kunsthaus Flora, Berlin); *A Midsummer Night's Dream, Angels & Demons* (Gründerzeit Museum, Berlin). As Assistant Director credits include: *Wollstonecraft Live!, Casanova* (Friedrichstadt Palast, Berlin); *Stillhalten* (Jewish Museum, Berlin).

Anna is the Artistic Director of Syndromus Theatre Company.

Nancy Meckler

Joint Artistic Director

Nancy Meckler became Artistic Director of Shared Experience in 1987, and was joined by Polly Teale in 1994. Previously she was a founder member of the Freehold Theatre and an Associate Director for Hampstead Theatre and the Leicester Haymarket.

Her award-winning productions for the company have toured widely in the UK and abroad. These include *The Tempest*, *Mother Courage* and *A Passage to India*. Also, five plays by Helen Edmundson: *Orestes*, *Anna Karenina*, *Gone to Earth*, *Mill on the Floss* and *War and Peace* (the last two co-directed with Polly Teale). She has directed *House of Desires*, *The Comedy of Errors* and *Romeo and Juliet* for the RSC and has recently directed *Aristo* by Martin Sherman at Chichester Festival Theatre.

Jon Harris

Administrative Producer

Jon is Shared Experience's Administrative Producer. Previously he was the founding Director of Stratford Circus, Director of Harlow Playhouse, and the New End Theatre, Hampstead. He is an Associate of Actorshop, an arts training and management consultancy.

Sharon John

Administrative Manager

Sharon has been with Shared Experience for almost three years. She trained as a Stage Manager at LAMDA. In the intervening years, her career has undergone a series of transmogrifications, until coming full circle and landing her back in the theatre.

Bailey Lock

Assistant Administrator

Bailey graduated from Durham University in 2004. She was formerly the administrator of Sphinx Theatre Company and is a script reader for the Old Vic and Soho Theatre. She produced *A Real Humane Person Who Cares and All That* by Adam Brace at this year's Edinburgh Festival.

Helen Hillman

Finance Officer

Helen has been part of Shared Experience for two years. She is also Casting Coordinator at Shakespeare's Globe and was Acting General Manager at Sphinx Theatre Company from November 2006 to December 2007. Helen is Producer of Adverse Camber, a theatre company she set up with Jacqui Somerville (Artistic Director), which had its first production at the Union Theatre, London in April 2006.

Kate Saxon

Associate Director

For Shared Experience: Associate Director of *Jane Eyre* and *After Mrs Rochester*, also responsible for the company's Youth and Education department.

As a freelance Director, credits include: *Far From The Madding Crowd* (English Touring Theatre); *Chains of Dew* (Orange Tree); *Arturo Ui* (Palace Theatre Watford); *Westminster Shorts* (Soho Theatre); *The French Lieutenant's Woman* (UK Tour/World Premiere, Fulton, USA); *Nine Parts of Desire* (Wilma, USA); *Hysteria*, *Humble Boy* (Northcott); *Caution Trousers*, *Clearing The Colours* (Stephen Joseph); *Trust Byron* (Gate); *Scratching The Façade* (Birmingham Rep/Symphony Hall); *La Bohème* (Opera North); *The Secret Garden* (Salisbury Playhouse); *The Little Prince*, *Grimm Tales* (ATY, Alaska).

FOR SHARED EXPERIENCE

SUPPORTED BY
**CITY OF
WESTMINSTER**

ARTS COUNCIL
ENGLAND

PAST PRODUCTIONS

SHARED EXPERIENCE

2008 *Ten Tiny Toes*
(co-production with Liverpool
Everyman & Playhouse),
War and Peace
(co-production with
Nottingham Playhouse
& Hampstead Theatre)

2007 *Kindertransport*

2006 *Orestes,*
Jane Eyre

2005 *Brontë*

2004 *A Passage to India,*
Gone to Earth

2003 *Madame Bovary,*
After Mrs Rochester

2002 *The Clearing,*
A Passage to India

2001 *Mill on the Floss,*
The Magic Toyshop
(director Rebecca Gatward)

2000 *Mother Courage*
& Her Children,
A Doll's House

1999 *Jane Eyre,*
The House of Bernarda Alba

1998 *Anna Karenina,*
I Am Yours (collaboration
with The Royal Court)

1997 *Jane Eyre*

1996 *The Tempest,*
War and Peace
(co-production with RNT)

1995 *Desire under the Elms,*
Mill on the Floss

1994 *The Danube,*
Mill on the Floss

1993 *Anna Karenina*

1992 *Trilby and Svengali,*
Anna Karenina

1991 *Sweet Sessions,*
The Closing Number
(director Mladen Materic)

1990 *The Birthday Party*

1989 *Abingdon Square,*
Heartbreak House,
True West

1988 *The Bacchae*

RECENT AWARDS

Kindertransport

Marion Bailey – **TMA Award 2007** nominated for Best Supporting Actress

Bo Barton – **Stage Management Association Award 2006** for Outstanding Achievement

A Passage to India

Manchester Evening News Theatre Award 2005 nominated for Best Visiting Production

Fenella Woolgar – **Manchester Evening News Theatre Award 2005** nominated for Best Actress in a Visiting Production

Gone to Earth

TMA/Opus Award 2004 nominated for Best Touring Production

After Mrs Rochester

Polly Teale – **Evening Standard Award 2003** for Best Director

Time Out Live Award 2004 for Best Play in the West End

Evening Standard Award 2003 nominated for Best Play

TMA/Opus Award 2003 nominated for Best Touring Production

Mill on the Floss

Helen Hayes Award 2002 for Outstanding Non-Resident Production in Washington DC

SUPPORT US

Become a Friend or Patron of Shared Experience

We hope you enjoy watching our work onstage. It's the result of an enormous amount of careful preparation, and represents only part of what we achieve.

Our productions come about as the result of a unique creative process led by our Joint Artistic Directors, Nancy Meckler and Polly Teale. We conduct an intensive period of collaboration through script commission, development and (at a later stage) workshops with performers. The writer works with the director and actors to evolve a visual and imaginative language for the particular piece. Our process is costly, but it's vital to assure the quality of what you see onstage.

Central to our work, in addition, are the activities of the Youth & Education department under the leadership of our Associate Director, Kate Saxon. We offer schools' workshops, pre-and post-show talks with members of the company, and our trademark "Inside Out" days at which school parties gain a unique insight into the production process.

We also have a Youth Theatre. Young performers, often from London's less socially-advantaged communities, come to stretch their imaginations in courses led by the company's artists.

By becoming a Friend or Patron of Shared Experience you directly help us to continue our commitment to excellence both onstage and in our work with young people in schools and our Youth Theatre, as well as enjoying the benefits set out on the following pages.

To discuss joining us please contact:

Jon Harris, Administrative Producer, Shared Experience
Tel: 020 7587 1596
Email: jon@sharedexperience.org.uk

www.sharedexperience.org.uk

FRIENDS

You can join Friends of Shared Experience at a variety of levels as follows:

Your donation	Min value to us after reclaiming *Gift Aid*＊	What your donation can do
£100	£125	Your gift pays for a drama student, or new entrant to the acting profession, to attend our unique two-day "Process Workshop"
£250	£312	Your gift funds our stage lighting budget for a single week's worth of shows
£500	£625	Your gift pays for a tutor to lead a Youth Theatre project for one week
£750	£937	Your gift pays for one costume for one actor in a Shared Experience production, and its upkeep through a production lasting several months

Benefits: we offer all Friends of Shared Experience:

• A complimentary copy of the programme of each production, posted directly to you as soon as the production opens.

• Invitation to our Annual Cocktail Party with our actors, held after a performance.

• Invitation to a private pre- or post-show discussion during every production we do.

• Advance information on all Shared Experience productions.

＊ Tax-efficient giving: we are a registered charity (no. 271414), so if you are a UK income tax payer you can take advantage of several measures designed to make your gift cost less and provide more.

• Gift Aid – for every £1 you give us, we reclaim an additional 25p directly from HMRC.

• Higher rate relief – if you a higher-rate taxpayer, then on the same £1, you reclaim 25p through your tax return. **Therefore a gift worth £1.25 to us has cost you only 75p**.

• Should you choose to let us have the benefit of your tax saving, we can receive £1.50 for your original £1.

PATRONS

Our patrons, whose number is limited to 100, agree to make a minimum donation of £1,000 per annum

Your donation	Min value to us after reclaiming *Gift Aid**	What your donation can do
£1,000	£1,250	Your gift pays for an Education Pack for a production – an invaluable resource for teachers and students
£2,000	£2,500	Your gift will pay for a Rehearsal Assistant on our Apprentice Scheme. A young entrant to the profession will gain a unique experience on one production
£3,000	£3,750	Your gift pays for a development workshop at which performers work on a new script
£5,000	£6,250	Your gift pays to commission a new script
£10,000	£12,500	Your gift pays for one actor to rehearse and perform in a Shared Experience production, lasting several months

Benefits: In addition to the Benefits which our Friends receive (see across), our Patrons are also offered:

- Access to a special complimentary ticket allocation held until 24 hours before each performance (available on a first come first served basis and restricted to two tickets), with complimentary interval drinks.

- Credit in our Annual report, Accounts and our corporate literature.

- Press releases and selected reviews of all our productions sent directly to you.

- An invitation, annually, to a special "Behind the Scenes" event. Working with leading actors who have performed with Shared Experience, our Artistic Directors conduct a special rehearsal Masterclass which gives a unique insight into how our work is made. It's an unforgettable evening which will change the way you look at theatre forever.

EDUCATION

Shared Experience's Youth & Education work is central to the company. All the productions are accompanied by an Education Programme, which is supported by Westminster City Council, in London and on tour.

Workshops
Suitable for Drama/English Literature students at: GCSE, A Level and in Higher Education. Two types of workshop are available to book:

- *Mine* – the rehearsal process and production

- Shared Experience Process – innovative and unique exercises from the rehearsal room

Post-Show Discussions
Offer a chance to stay behind after a performance to meet the cast for Q & A. Contact your theatre box office to check the date.

YOUTH THEATRE

Our Youth Theatre is a place where young performers come to stretch their imaginations in courses led by artists from within the company. The Youth Theatre runs a variety of workshops and projects designed to put members in touch with the physical style of the main company's work.

There will be a specially commissioned project for the Youth Theatre, exploring themes around *Mine*, which will be rehearsed and performed in the Autumn. Any interested young person aged 14 - 22 can join.

For more information on any of the above please contact Shared Experience by email at **bailey@sharedexperience.org.uk**

HampsteadTheatre

Hampstead Theatre is not only a magnificent, purpose-built, state-of-the-art theatre that has just celebrated its fifth birthday, but a company fast approaching its fiftieth with a particular mission: to find, develop, and produce new plays to the highest possible standards, for as many people as we can encourage to see them.

Our work remains rooted in our community, but is both national and international in its scope and ambition. Occasionally, we will do a revival of an old play, but only when there is an artistic and financial imperative to do so.

The list of playwrights who had their early work produced at Hampstead Theatre, who are now filling theatres all over the country and beyond include: Simon Block, Michael Frayn, Brian Friel, Terry Johnson, Dennis Kelly, Hanif Kureishi, Mike Leigh, Abi Morgan, Rona Munro, Tamsin Oglesby, Harold Pinter, Philip Ridley, Shelagh Stephenson, debbie tucker green, Crispin Whittell and Roy Williams.

Hampstead Theatre also supports a successful integrated creative learning programme that gives people, and young people in particular, the opportunity to participate in a range of writing and performance projects.

We are supported by public funding, the philanthropy of the private sector and our box office.

The 50th anniversary in 2009 will be a year of celebrations and this is an exciting time to be part of Hampstead Theatre.

Artistic Director **Anthony Clark**
Executive Director **Rebecca Morland**

Hampstead Theatre gratefully acknowledges the support of

Hampstead Theatre would like to thank the following Corporate Partners, Trusts & Foundations for supporting our creativity:

Acacia Charitable Trust, The Andor Charitable Trust, Arimathea Charitable Trust, Arts & Business, Auerbach Trust Charity, Austin & Hope Pilkington Trust, Bank Leumi, The Basil Samuels Charitable Trust, The Big Lottery, Bennetts Associates, Blick Rothenberg, Britten-Pears Foundation, The Chapman Charitable Trust, The Columbia Foundation, Coutts Charitable Trust, Denton Wilde Sapte Charitable Trust, D'Oyly Carte Charitable Trust, Duis Charitable Trust, Equitable Charitable Trust, The Eranda Foundation, The Ernest Cook Trust, Nicole Farhi, Fenton Arts Award, The Gerald Ronson Foundation, Goethe-Institut, The Hampstead & Highgate Express, Hampstead Wells and Campden Trust, Harold Hyam Wingate Foundation, The Jack Petchey Foundation, John Lyon's Charity, Kennedy Leigh Charitable Trust, Knight Frank, Linbury Trust, Mackintosh Foundation, Michael Marks Charitable Trust, Milly Apthorp Charitable Trust, The Morel Trust, The Noël Coward Foundation, The N Smith Charitable Trust, Nyman Libson Paul, The Paul Hamlyn Foundation, Pembertons Property Management, Prince's Foundation for Children and the Arts, PRS Foundation, The Rayne Foundation, Reed Elsevier, Royal Victoria Hall Foundation, Salans, Samuel French, Savills, The Shoresh Foundation, Solomon Taylor & Shaw, Sweet and Maxwell, The Vandervell Foundation, Charles Wolfson Foundation, Zurich Community Trust.

For more information please contact Lucy French
at **Lucyf@hampsteadtheatre.com** or on **020 7449 4158**.

www.hampsteadtheatre.com

Polly Teale

MINE

NICK HERN BOOKS
www.nickhernbooks.co.uk

SHARED EXPERIENCE
www.sharedexperience.org.uk

For Mary

Author's Note

The Man and Woman's home is an exquisite, minimalist, architect-designed house. Lots of glass and white with the occasional piece of sculptural furniture. More like a house in a dream with vast spaces, the furniture like islands in the expanse of white.

There is also a large doll's house, once magnificent, but fallen into disrepair. A relic of the Woman's childhood.

The Child exists in the Woman's head and cannot be seen by the other characters. She represents different things to the Woman at different times. Sometimes she represents the child the Woman longs for and a mythic, idealised sense of childhood lost. Sometimes she is a memory, a ghost of herself as a child. She also functions as an inner child, expressing the Woman's repressed feelings or even her fears about what the baby might become. Sometimes these overlap and fuse.

 The original Shared Experience production also used video projections to express the Woman's unconscious, her fears and fantasies.

In the projected imagery there are three landscapes. One is the interior of an old house, with endless corridors and doors, which relates to the dilapidated doll's house and her dream that she is trapped inside. The doll's house, of course, is a relic of her unhappy childhood and a part of the self.

The second landscape is a wood with a river. This relates to a place the Woman escaped to as a child. Wild and beautiful, it has a heightened sense of something elemental that has been lost. A mythic notion of childhood. A state of unfettered freedom, connected to nature. The antithesis of the home she has created for herself as an adult.

Finally there is the landscape of the city. Dirty, threatening, sometimes beautiful. This imagery relates to the Woman's feelings about Rose and the world she inhabits; she is both repelled and fascinated by it. Again, it is the antithesis of the couple's exquisite, architect-designed home, with its immaculate interior and manicured garden.

I have made occasional references to the projected images in the script, although the play can be performed without this element.

Thanks

Thanks to David Annen, Harriet Balsom, Aveca Chasteauneuf, Glemham Hall, Gill Gray, Mick Meaghan, Lucy Richardson, Eden Rickson, Natalie Salaman, Michael Simmons, Jeremy Swift, Jane Temple and all the actors who took part in the *Mine* workshops.

Polly Teale

Mine was first performed by Shared Experience at Warwick Arts Centre on 2 October 2008 and premiered in London at Hampstead Theatre on 9 October 2008. The cast was as follows:

MOTHER	Marion Bailey
SISTER/KATYA	Clare Lawrence Moody
MAN	Alistair Petrie
ROSE	Lorraine Stanley
WOMAN	Katy Stephens
CHILD	Sophie Stone

Other parts played by members of the company.

Director	Polly Teale
Designer	Angela Simpson
Music and Sound Designer	Peter Salem
Company Movement	Liz Ranken
Lighting Designer	Colin Greenfell
Video/Projection Designer	Thomas Gray for The Gray Circle

Characters

WOMAN
MAN
Woman's MOTHER
Woman's younger SISTER

KATYA, *their housekeeper*
SOCIAL WORKER
ROSE, *the baby's birth mother*
CHILD, *exists only in the Woman's mind*

REMOVAL MEN
DINNER GUEST
DIRECTOR *and* CAMERAPERSON

A forward slash (/) indicates the point at which the next speaker interrupts.

This text went to press before the end of rehearsals and so may differ slightly from the play as performed.

ACT ONE

A WOMAN *is sitting in her study, with her laptop. It is late evening. She is in the middle of a phone call. She reads from the screen in front of her.*

WOMAN. In a frantic world home should be a sanctuary, comma, a cocoon, comma, a place of retreat, full stop. Home is a world of our own making, full stop. A world that expresses who we are and what we believe, full stop. Home is a place of the spirit, comma, of the imagination, comma, where anything is possible, full stop. Here we are free to dream, semi-colon; to create our own reality, full stop.

A MAN *is standing, listening, in the doorway.*

MAN. Your supper's cold.

WOMAN (*still on the phone*). Tomorrow evening. We're going to shoot the garden candlelit. It's the last photo. The final page. Pray it doesn't rain. (*Putting her hand over the receiver.*) Sorry. (*Into the phone.*) Not tonight. In the morning. I'll send that through now… Got to go.

She puts down the phone.

Sorry.

MAN. You said you were nearly finished an hour ago.

WOMAN. Let me send this then I'm through.

MAN. I need to talk to you.

WOMAN. It was supposed to be proofed on Tuesday. Been on the phone all day.

MAN. I know. I tried to call.

WOMAN. Nightmare with the final shoot. Man next door won't let us use the crane. Offered him a grand, but he still says 'no'. It's the only way to get the sculpture into the garden. They're trying to sort a helicopter. Technically he can't object as it won't touch the ground, and the air, it seems, belongs to no one.

MAN (*indicating the laptop*). Turn it off.

WOMAN. Ten minutes. Just let me get this done.

MAN. Now.

WOMAN. Five minutes. I promise. She's waiting for it.

MAN. I had a call today. This evening.

WOMAN. Tell me when I'm through.

MAN (*slowly*). They rang to say…

  Silence.

WOMAN. What? What happened?

MAN. They've had a referral.

  Beat.

WOMAN. What did they say?

MAN. We're going in tomorrow morning to talk it / through.

WOMAN. Why didn't you tell me? Why didn't they call me?

MAN. They did. They couldn't get through.

WOMAN. Why didn't you call as soon as / you heard?

MAN. I did. You were engaged. I left three messages.

WOMAN. What did they say? When? How soon can / we…

MAN. Tomorrow, they'll tell us more.

WOMAN. Oh my God.

  They hold one another.

MAN. I've moved my consultation so I can come.

WOMAN. I'll ring my agent. She'll have to get me out of New York next week.

MAN. Let's wait until we've had the meeting.

WOMAN. Tomorrow night. The final shoot.

MAN. The meeting's at ten in the morning. We'll be done by midday.

WOMAN. I'll cancel *Rigoletto*, and the private view. You can't go to Switzerland. The boxroom. We can clear it at the weekend.

MAN. Hang on.

WOMAN. We'll need a skip, and a man and –

MAN. A skip?

WOMAN. Clear the junk. I'll phone my mother. Cancel Sunday.

MAN. I don't think we should start changing things. Not yet.

WOMAN. I'll tell them I can't make New York. They'll have to cope.

She picks up the phone. He takes it from her.

MAN. Wait a minute.

Beat.

WOMAN. What did they say? Tell me everything you know.

MAN. We mustn't get too…

WOMAN. What? (*Pause.*) Too what?

MAN. I just don't want you to be… disappointed. Don't think we should… I think we should try to stay…

WOMAN. Try to stay… what? As if nothing's happened? (*Beat.*) As if we're told every day we might be about to meet… to meet our…

She can't say it.

MAN. We don't know yet. We need to look at all the information. Assess the chances of / … problems.

WOMAN. Five years. Ten if you start at the beginning. Twenty if I go back to the day I first wanted... first knew I...

MAN. It's a girl.

WOMAN. A girl.

The CHILD *appears, about ten years old. She covers her eyes and starts to count as if playing hide-and-seek. She counts as the dialogue continues.*

MAN. A baby girl. Three weeks, two days old. The mother's young. Her first child. She didn't present until the birth.

WOMAN. A girl.

MAN. She's in hospital. In detox. So far there's no obvious malfunction. She's tested negative for HIV. No sign of foetal alcohol syndrome in the face, although you can't always tell straight away. Her MRI looks / normal.

WOMAN. She's here. She's somewhere in this city. Out there in the dark. Breathing. Alive.

They hug.

Lights change. The WOMAN *takes over the count from the* CHILD. *The* CHILD *hides under the* WOMAN's *chair.*

WOMAN. Eighteen. Nineteen. Nineteen and a half. Nineteen and three-quarters... Twenty. (*Shouts.*) Coming, ready or not. (*Starts to search.*) Is she behind the door? (*Looks behind the door.*) No. Or is she under the stool? (*Looks under the stool.*) Then she must be behind the chair.

The CHILD *crawls out, laughing, and runs away.*

Projected image of a CHILD *running along a corridor, through doors and then out into a forest.*

Lights change. The following morning. A meeting room at the adoption centre.

SOCIAL WORKER. So that's just about everything we know. Obviously, we're going to give Rose as much support as we can. She says she's going to fight it. She wants to go into rehab. Wants contact as often as possible. She'll have to prove she can handle it.

MAN. And the father?

SOCIAL WORKER. She won't talk about him. She might not know who he is, of course, or if she does, she wants to forget.

MAN (*reading from the file*). No visible sign of FAS. Tested negative for HIV, but there are increased chances of Hepatitis B, which can't be detected until eighteen months?

The SOCIAL WORKER *nods.*

The mother a category-three offender, which means the baby will go through withdrawal during detox.

WOMAN. What is she like? The mother.

SOCIAL WORKER. Depends. Doesn't talk much, but she's bright. Lucid. Knows what's going on. Doesn't trust anyone, but that's hardly surprising. Neither would you if you'd lived her life. As I said, she can be violent, especially if she's been drinking. She won't be allowed contact if she's been drinking. That's one of the conditions.

MAN. In your opinion. I know you can't say for sure, but what do you think are the chances... I mean, how likely, how possible is it that she'll...

SOCIAL WORKER. Turn it around?

The MAN *nods.*

Unlikely. I mean, purely statistically. She's been using since she was a teenager. It's her life. But it's not impossible. She's not stupid and she knows... she knows this is her last chance.

WOMAN. What do you mean?

SOCIAL WORKER. If she carries on the way she is she won't
be here. You can only live so long like that. If the drugs
and the drink don't do it then someone else will. The
money for the drugs, she gets it the way most of these
women do –

WOMAN. You mean –

SOCIAL WORKER. She's a sex worker. A prostitute.

MAN (*reading the form*). No permanent address. What does
that mean exactly?

SOCIAL WORKER. Could be sleeping in a hostel or there
might be a boyfriend or somewhere she –

MAN. Homeless?

SOCIAL WORKER. Officially.

MAN. And she won't be given custody unless that changes. It's
a legal requirement. An address. Her own address.

SOCIAL WORKER. That will be part of the rehab programme.
The final stage. (*Begins to pack her bag.*) It can be harder
than you think. People who've been homeless don't always
find it easy to adapt.

WOMAN. How do you mean?

SOCIAL WORKER. When I worked in housing. We'd spend
months getting someone a flat. Get it kitted out. They're
made up. Everything's going to be different. A new beginning. Fresh start. Next thing I know they've flooded it or
burnt the place down. It's as if they don't believe it's possible for them. It's easier to destroy it than to try, to try to
make a home, a life, and fail. We had one man slept outside
on the balcony. Said he didn't like the walls. (*Gets up.*) I'll
leave you to read it through. You've got until Friday to make
a decision. If there's anything you want to ask, ring me. I'm
sure you'll find there are lots more questions once you've
had a chance to talk –

WOMAN. We want her. I mean, we don't need to wait until Friday. We'd like to go ahead.

MAN. We'll look at the file.

The CHILD *enters, dragging a moth-eaten doll. She sits at the* WOMAN*'s feet.*

SOCIAL WORKER. There's a lot to think about. Give it a day to –

WOMAN. No. There isn't. We want her. You can tell them we… we'd like to proceed. We've said 'yes'. We'd like to begin as soon as possible.

SOCIAL WORKER. Well, that's great. I think you should take tomorrow to be sure you've made the right / decision.

MAN. Of course. We'll ring you on Friday morning.

WOMAN. When can we see her?

SOCIAL WORKER. Soon. We'll organise a visit with the hospital.

The CHILD *leads the* WOMAN *to the doll's house.*

Lights change. Late that night. The boxroom. There is the large, dilapidated doll's house. Once magnificent, it was left for years in a garage and has suffered damp and mildew. The CHILD *takes an aeroplane from a heap and flies it round the room. The* MAN *is standing in the doorway, watching. He does not see the* CHILD*. The* WOMAN *picks up the doll that the* CHILD *was carrying. She takes it to the doll's house. She opens the doll's house to reveal its interior, with furniture in disarray. She starts to pick up the tiny chairs and arrange them around a table. The* CHILD *leans in through the roof.*

WOMAN. I'd spend hours rearranging the furniture. It was my favourite place in all the world. Used to dream about it. Dream I was living inside it. Like it had grown or I'd shrunk and it was real. Like it had come to life and everything was just exactly as it was in the doll's house. Like the food was stuck on the plates and the drawers wouldn't open and the flowers in the wallpaper were huge. And the others, the others were dolls. I'm the only one who's real and... I want to go downstairs. I want to get out, but I remember, I realise that there are no stairs. There were no stairs. You can't get down. Get out.

The MAN *holds her mobile phone, and is reading a text.*

MAN. There's a message. 'Photos divine. Garden looks like heaven. Will e-mail images in morning.' She's trying to talk you into New York.

WOMAN. What does she say?

MAN. They're offering twice the fee.

WOMAN. Let me see.

He shows her the text.

I could come straight back on the red eye. Go there and back in a day.

The MAN *texts back.*

MAN. Done.

The CHILD *has come to sit at the* WOMAN*'s feet. She takes the doll and starts to play with it.*

WOMAN. When we first moved in... I used to come in here, daydream. Imagine myself telling stories. Singing songs. Think about the wallpaper. The colour scheme. Where to put the cot and the doll's house. And then... I stopped coming in and you started to put junk in here. The things we didn't want but felt guilty about throwing out. And then one day you called it the boxroom and after a while I called it the boxroom, even though I never came in here, couldn't come in here.

The CHILD *has started to sing to the doll.*

CHILD. Hush little baby, don't say a word,
        Mama's going to buy you a mockingbird...

The CHILD *continues to sing the song under the dialogue.*

WOMAN (*to the* MAN). Can you believe it? Can you believe she'll be here?

MAN (*kissing her forehead*). I'm going back to the studio.

WOMAN. Tonight?

MAN. The house in Switzerland. There's a problem with the windows. I need to look at the plans.

WOMAN. What's the matter?

MAN. Don't wait up. I'll set the alarm.

WOMAN. What is it?

MAN. I'm fine. I just need to check the dimensions. Some confusion.

She goes to him, puts her arms around him.

WOMAN. Tell me.

Pause.

MAN. I keep thinking about where she's been. The baby.

WOMAN. 'Been'?

MAN. All the things that must have happened while…

WOMAN. She's been in the hospital.

MAN. Before. When she was… Can you imagine? Can we even begin to imagine that woman's life?

WOMAN. There's no point.

MAN. It said there were bruises on her. Not just from the needles, but… all over. As if she'd been –

WOMAN. I don't want to know.

MAN. All over her body.

WOMAN. You shouldn't read all that… What use is it?

MAN. It happened.

WOMAN. It's over. There's nothing we can do about it. We have to start from here.

MAN. Why didn't she get an abortion? I mean, for Christ's sake, what did she think she was going to do with it?

WOMAN. Her.

MAN. What sort of life? How the hell does she think she's going to give it a life?

WOMAN. Her. She wants her. It's not rational. Not reasonable. It doesn't mean she's capable of looking after her. She wants a baby just like we want a baby. A little girl. A beautiful little baby girl.

The CHILD *puts the doll to bed, tucking her up and kissing her goodnight.*

Lights change. The WOMAN *is with her* MOTHER.

MOTHER. I just don't want you to get… burnt.

WOMAN. What?

MOTHER. It's hard enough with your own children.

WOMAN. What's that got to do with anything?

MOTHER. She's being taken away because the mother is ill.

WOMAN. She's had a difficult life.

MOTHER. Whatever you call it, it means the same thing. Problems.

WOMAN. Do you think we haven't / thought…

MOTHER. I know. I know you know. And I know you've read all the books and looked it up on the internet and talked to your friend who's a consultant whatever. But what will it be like? What will it actually be like, waiting and watching and knowing that any day now this perfect little baby is going to –

WOMAN. Perfect. What's perfect? Is it not worth raising a child if they're not going to be perfect?

MOTHER. That's not what I / said.

WOMAN. Cleverest. Best. Most successful.

MOTHER. I didn't say that.

WOMAN. You meant it.

MOTHER. What are you trying to say?

WOMAN. Forget it.

MOTHER. There's nothing wrong with wanting the best for your children. Don't ask me to be ashamed of that. I know what it's like to have nothing. To come from nothing.

WOMAN. Let's leave it.

MOTHER. I know the value of success.

WOMAN. I don't want to argue.

MOTHER. I'm just not sure you know what you're letting yourself in for. Not sure you have any idea –

WOMAN. What does anyone know when a baby's born what the future holds? What might be hidden in their genes, in their tiny body. There isn't an insurance policy. There's nothing we can do to guarantee happiness, health, any of the things that really matter.

MOTHER. This isn't any baby. This is the baby of someone who's abused their body in every possible way. Someone who didn't have a single check-up during her pregnancy. Someone / whose –

WOMAN. How do you know?

MOTHER. I read it.

WOMAN. That's private.

MOTHER. Then it shouldn't be lying on the table.

WOMAN. When I saw the photo, don't know why, I had this desire to show it to you. I thought she looked so beautiful, that surely you'd change your mind. Surely you couldn't / fail to be…

MOTHER. Okay, so perhaps you'll be lucky and she's fine and there's only the future to worry about. The possibility that one day, perhaps… But what if you're unlucky and there are problems here and now? Things that won't go away. That will get worse. Things that mean you have to change your lovely life –

WOMAN. Oh God.

MOTHER. – Get your hands dirty.

WOMAN. Mother.

MOTHER. Step out of your ivory tower and live in the real world where things are messy and frustrating and disappointing and –

WOMAN. 'Ivory tower.'

MOTHER. You have a very privileged existence.

WOMAN. You have no idea.

MOTHER. Always have.

WOMAN. Where have you been for the last four years? What do you think it's been like, waking up every day knowing that the one, the only thing in the world you really want, you can't have? After the last time. The last attempt. The day I got my period. It was Christmas Day, actually, and you were there and everybody. All the children opening presents and I was late. Three wonderful, ecstatic, delirious weeks late. And I was watching and imagining…

The CHILD *stands behind her. She puts her hands over the* WOMAN*'s eyes.*

I let myself imagine.

The CHILD *hugs her from behind.*

It was as if I'd made it happen. Made it come. Because I'd allowed myself, for a moment. For an hour or maybe two to think it was possible. That maybe this time...

The WOMAN *turns to embrace the* CHILD. *The* CHILD *runs away, laughing.*

Lights change. The WOMAN *and the* MAN *at home.*

WOMAN. The worst thing is, everything she said, it's true. Of course I'm terrified there'll be something wrong with her. And I'm afraid I won't love her enough because she isn't mine and she doesn't look like me or you or any of us and I'm too selfish just like she thinks I am –

MAN. Stop it.

WOMAN. Or worse than that.

MAN. Shshsh.

WOMAN. We fall in love with her, completely and utterly, and then they take her away. Take her back.

MAN. Listen –

WOMAN. Or later, when she's older, she gets ill, or sick, sick like her mother. Messed up, miserable, wretched, because there's something in there. In the genes. Like a curse in a fairy story that you can't break no matter how much you love her, no matter how hard you try to give her everything... to make her better... She's right. I want a perfect little girl. I want her to be beautiful and clever and happy and gorgeous and talented and –

MAN. We don't have to... We haven't agreed. We could still...

WOMAN. What?

MAN. Say no.

WOMAN. No?

MAN. If it's not right. If it doesn't feel right.

Beat.

WOMAN. I can't believe you said that.

MAN. You said –

WOMAN. I said. I said I was afraid. That doesn't mean I'm
    going to –

MAN. Okay.

WOMAN. I thought you wanted…

MAN. I do. I –

WOMAN. I thought. I thought you said –

MAN. I did. I just… I don't know.

WOMAN. When we found out I wasn't pregnant. The last time.
    And you said it was like a death. Like a child had died. Our
    child had… Like there was no future. Like it had collapsed
    overnight. Everything you'd imagined. Gone. Everything
    we'd built was for nothing. For no one.

Pause.

This is it. This is what we wanted. What we've been waiting
for. This is our chance.

MAN. I know. I…

WOMAN. I want to see her so much, I ache all over. I can't
    sleep. Can't eat. Can't think about anything but… her. Of
    course I'm afraid. It's terrifying. But there isn't a choice.

The CHILD, *humming the lullaby, wraps the doll in a
blanket, puts it into the* WOMAN's *arms, and leaves.*

Lights change. In the hospital, on the first visit. The WOMAN
holds the baby in silence.

WOMAN. She's looking at me. Look at her eyes. She's… beau-
    tiful… aren't you… beautiful.

We become aware of ROSE, *the birth mother of the baby,
standing a few feet away, watching. There is a sense of threat,*

*of danger, like an animal whose young are being touched by
an interloper. Her objective in the scene is to undermine their
sense of entitlement to the baby and assert her own.*

ROSE. Yes. She is.

WOMAN. Thank you.

Pause.

ROSE. Perfect.

WOMAN. Yes.

ROSE. The most perfect thing ever.

Pause.

WOMAN. How old is yours? Which one is yours?

ROSE. She's four weeks. Two days, three hours and – (*Looking
at her watch.*) thirty minutes.

WOMAN. Is she doing well?

ROSE. Beautiful. She's beautiful.

The baby starts to cry.

MAN. If you don't mind we… It's our first visit and we'd like to –

ROSE. I know.

MAN. We don't have very long and we'd like to be alone.

ROSE. I know. It's the same for me. Goes past so quick, don't
it. Feels like no time at all. Like you've only just arrived and
it's over. They're telling you it's over.

MAN. I'm sorry. I don't want to be rude, but we really –

ROSE. Don't want to be rude. No, you shouldn't be rude. Not
to me.

They stare at her, uncertain.

I come because I wanted to meet you. Wanted to be here
when you… There's things you should know. I need to tell

you. She don't like being laid on her back, you see. That's why she's crying. She likes to be up so's she can see what's going on. Do you mind if I show you, because that's the easiest way, isn't it.

ROSE *takes the baby and holds her on her shoulder. The crying subsides.*

That's it. That's better. There's a good girl. Shshsh. She's all right now, see. I was the oldest of nine so I got lots of prac- tice. My folks were out most of the time. Left it to me, so you see, I know about babies. About children. There's nothing I don't know about kids.

MAN (*getting up*). I'll go and get –

ROSE. No, don't do that. She's all right now. She can smell me, can't she. They say that, don't they. They can smell you. Hear your voice. All them months inside, listening to you. Strange to think she was inside me only a few weeks ago. Sometimes wish she was still there. Miss her, don't I, giving me indigestion, keeping me awake at night. Making me sick.

Magic, int it? Like a miracle, what grows in there. Not just skin, but nails and hair and eyelashes and perfect little ears, like seashells. Purple, she were, when she come out. Like part of your insides. Part of you ripped out. All them days, weeks, months spent wondering what she'd look like, and here she is. Here you are. Only you can't tell yet, can you. Takes years, don't it… to become… themselves. To see who they're going to be. To know who they are.

MAN. Look. I'm sure you mean well, but I… we… weren't expecting –

WOMAN (*to the* MAN). It's okay.

MAN. You're not supposed to be here, are you?

ROSE. 'Not supposed'?

MAN. You'd be in trouble if they knew.

ROSE. I'm her mother.

MAN. It's up to you. You can leave now or I'm going to get –

WOMAN. Don't.

ROSE *leans forward to shake their hands with her free arm.*

ROSE. Rose. I know your names. They told me. You're going to foster her until I'm ready –

MAN. I'm going to go and get our social worker.

WOMAN. It's all right.

MAN (*to the* WOMAN). I don't think we should get involved.

ROSE. Not get involved. She's my baby.

MAN (*to* ROSE). Either you leave now or I'm going.

The baby starts to cry. The MAN *goes.*

ROSE. She's hungry. Ready for her feed. Two o'clock.

WOMAN. Yes. They said we could. Left us a bottle.

ROSE. I wanted to feed her myself, but they said I couldn't. Gave me pills to dry it up, but I didn't take them. It leaks out when she cries. I think she can smell it. Like an animal, isn't it. You realise that, when you have a baby. We're animals. Things happen. Nothing to do with you. It's the body. Takes over. The instinct. Don't seem fair, does it. I got it. She wants it, but they won't let me give it to her.

WOMAN. Rose.

ROSE. Won't let me.

WOMAN. We…

ROSE. They won't let me.

WOMAN. We want you to know we will take the very best care of her for you. We will try to do, try to give her what you would want.

ROSE. What I want. What I want. You think this is what I want. Them taking her away. Taking her away from me. Somewhere I don't know. Can't find her. Can't see her.

WOMAN. I'm sorry. I know this must be very hard.

ROSE. I undress her. Look at her body. Try to remember. To learn her by heart. Everything. Every detail, so's when she's gone I'll be able to imagine. Imagine I'm holding her. Feel her weight. Her smell. See her weird little toes. The soft hair on her back. Like a monkey. The birthmark on her cheek. Then I think maybe I shouldn't, in case I miss her too much and I can't stand it and I wish I never saw her. Never smelt, felt, touched. But it's too late now. I done it, haven't I. Let her in. Let her into me.

The MAN *returns with the* SOCIAL WORKER.

SOCIAL WORKER (*gently*). Rose. You know you're not allowed to be here this afternoon, don't you?

ROSE. Aren't I?

SOCIAL WORKER. Ten till one. That's what we agreed.

ROSE. I forgot.

SOCIAL WORKER. If you want to see the baby you have to stick to / what we agreed…

ROSE. S'all right. I'm going now.

SOCIAL WORKER. We can arrange a meeting like we said we would.

ROSE. S'all right. I'm going. (*Whispers.*) Bye bye, my beautiful. My sweet. Bye bye, darling. Mummy be back tomorrow. Mummy loves you. Everything's going to be all right.

The CHILD *comes in, humming the lullaby.* ROSE *puts the baby into the bassinet and tucks her up. She kisses her on the forehead, goes to leave. The* CHILD *is at her side. The* WOMAN *stands.*

WOMAN. Rose. I hope we'll meet again soon.

ROSE. Do you?

WOMAN. I know this isn't what you hoped. What you wanted.

ROSE. No.

WOMAN. I'm sorry. I'm…

ROSE. Sorry. Yes. So am I.

ROSE *and the* CHILD *leave*.

Lights change. The next day. The WOMAN*'s* SISTER *has arrived carrying a large box of baby stuff. She is unpacking it, showing the* WOMAN *the contents. The room has French windows, which look out over the garden where the* SISTER*'s children are playing*.

SISTER. That's the steriliser. That bit goes on top. And that goes… (*Can't work it out*.) There are instructions some-where. And a mobile. It's lost a rabbit, but it still goes round. The cot's in pieces in the car. I'll bring it in. Hope it's all there. If you get stuck, ring Robert. (*Shouting out of the windows at the children*.) Don't throw earth! Joe, stop it. Let him go. Take it in turns or I'll take it away. (*To the* WOMAN.) I'm sorry, they've thrown mud into the pool. I told them not to go near it. They've been ghastly all weekend. Thank God for Monday. Daniel broke Ben's iPod yesterday. So Ben took the batteries out of Dan's PSP and flushed them down the toilet, which is now blocked. Left Robert arguing with the emergency plumber about the call-out charge. A hundred and fifty pounds before he's even looked at it because it's Sunday… Ben's being bullied at school. Came home with a bloody lip. Tried to pretend he'd fallen over. Dad says he'll pay for him to go to Colfe's, but Robert won't hear a word of it. Thinks Dad's shaming him, which he probably is. Last time we went for supper, Dad took him into the new conservatory. After half an hour boring him to death about insulation levels and PVC, he gave him the 'winners and losers' speech. You can imagine how well that went down.

WOMAN. Oh dear!

SISTER. 'When I started selling double glazing, no one knew what it was.'

The SISTER *gets out a baby sling.*

That's one of those things earth-mother types wrap round themselves. Need half an hour and the instruction leaflet every time you put it on.

She lifts up a large carrier bag.

And there's a bag of clothes.

She gets a babygro out; it looks a bit grey, misshapen.

Just pass on anything you don't like the look of.

WOMAN. I'm not sure yet what we'll need.

SISTER. I expect you'll be buying new stuff.

WOMAN. Thank you. It's very thoughtful. I'll look through.

SISTER. Don't feel you have to. If it's not right. You probably won't want –

WOMAN. The cot. We bought one on Saturday. And a steriliser. Sorry. I should have said.

SISTER. It was just a thought. I wasn't sure whether… with your not knowing for definite… for certain… if she'll stay.

WOMAN (*changing the subject*). I'm going to get the doll's house restored. I've found photos of the day we got it. Do you remember? The year the business took off. Dad turned up at school in the new Daimler. Took us to Harrods for tea. 'You can choose anything. Anything you like.' I thought it was the most beautiful thing I'd ever seen. Do you remember? It had real window panes and shutters and chandeliers you could switch on and off.

SISTER. You wouldn't let me near it. I had to wait till you were out. Put everything back exactly how it was.

WOMAN (*looking out of the window*). Oh dear. They've trampled the allium. They're trying to climb –

SISTER (*shouting out of the window*). Don't touch the water sculpture. Just go to the other end of the garden and ignore her. If I have to come outside you'll be sorry.

Silence.

(*To the* WOMAN.) We'd love to come to the hospital and meet her... when you're ready.

WOMAN. Of course.

SISTER. She looks adorable in the photo.

WOMAN. She is.

SISTER. You all right?

WOMAN. Fine. I'm fine.

The SISTER *suddenly runs to the window.*

SISTER. Oh my God. What's he doing? (*Shouts.*) Daniel. Get down immediately. You're soaking. All of you, get in the car. Now. I don't care whose fault it is.

She gathers her bag, picks up the steriliser.

You'll ring, won't you, if there's anything we can do, and let us know when we can...

Kisses the WOMAN *goodbye.*

And ring Mum. Please. She was on the phone for an hour. I put her on speakerphone while I made supper. Don't think she noticed. (*Looking out of the window.*) Sorry about the... (*Indicates the trampled garden.*)

WOMAN. Don't worry. The gardener comes tomorrow. Give him something to do.

The SISTER *leaves.*

The CHILD *stands watching as the* WOMAN *winds up the mobile. As it starts to play, the* CHILD *takes the mobile out of her hand and holds it. The battery is low and the tune limps along.*

Lights change. A room at the adoption centre. ROSE *sits opposite the* MAN *and the* WOMAN. *She is restless, uneasy, avoiding eye contact.*

SOCIAL WORKER (*to* ROSE). So, this is your opportunity to ask any questions you might have. (*Pause.*) Or you might have things you'd like to say.

ROSE. No thank you.

SOCIAL WORKER. Tomorrow the baby –

ROSE. Beauty.

SOCIAL WORKER. Tomorrow she'll be leaving the hospital and going to stay with –

ROSE. I know. You told me.

SOCIAL WORKER. As we agreed you'll have contact every Monday and Wednesday at eleven o'clock. For two hours, here at the unit. If for any reason you can't come / or you…

ROSE. I can.

SOCIAL WORKER. There's a number on the back for you to ring –

ROSE. I can come.

SOCIAL WORKER. We'll wait for an hour / and then…

ROSE. You won't. You won't have to wait. I told you. I'll be here.

SOCIAL WORKER. Good. That's good.

WOMAN. We'll keep a diary of how she's sleeping and feeding. Anything significant that she does. We'll let you know what she weighs / each time she's –

ROSE. Can I go now?

SOCIAL WORKER. I know this is very difficult for you. I know it's not what you hoped –

ROSE. I said, can I go?

WOMAN. Are you sure there's nothing you want to –

ROSE (*standing*). I'm sure.

WOMAN (*standing*). Thank you for coming. I hope, over the next few months we'll be able to… work together to give her –

ROSE. Beauty.

WOMAN. – to give Beauty the best possible start. I want you to feel you can ask us whatever… That we're here to / help.

ROSE. I bought her something.

She gets something out of her pocket. It is an identity bracelet.

It's got her name on it. I want her to wear it. I want you to promise me that she'll wear it. Always.

WOMAN. I promise. We promise.

ROSE *puts the bracelet into the* WOMAN*'s hand and goes to the door to leave. As she is about to exit:*

MAN. It's not safe.

ROSE *turns.*

It's unsafe for a baby to wear jewellery.

ROSE. It's an identity bracelet. It locks.

MAN. I can see what it is.

SOCIAL WORKER (*to the* MAN). Can we talk about this later?

ROSE. You said I could ask you. 'Whatever,' she said. She just said it. Just now.

WOMAN. Thank you, Rose.

MAN. It's dangerous.

ROSE. It's a bracelet.

MAN. Babies can choke. Can die.

ROSE. You think I don't know that? You think I'm stupid. You think I'm going to give her something that will harm her.

MAN. I'm sure that wasn't your intention, however –

ROSE. What do you know? What the hell do you know? In your expensive suit with your winter tan and your fuck-off Rolex and your perfect wife. What the fuck would you know about babies? About what would harm a baby?

SOCIAL WORKER. Rose. Calm down.

WOMAN. Thank you. Thank you, Rose. It's beautiful. She is beautiful.

ROSE. I want you to call her by her name.

WOMAN. We will.

Lights change. The MAN *and the* WOMAN *are at home.*

MAN. Are you serious?

WOMAN. It's her name.

MAN. Her name! You mean it's written on some tacky identity bracelet.

WOMAN. She chose it.

MAN. Like a cattle tag. Like she's been branded with her owner's initials. She'll be wanting her ears pierced next. Then her belly button.

WOMAN. We don't have to use all of it. We could call her Bea or… Bew… or Beau.

MAN. Bow!

WOMAN. Beau. It's French. French for… lovely.

MAN. Beauty. It's not even a name. When did you ever hear of anyone –

WOMAN. Sleeping Beauty. Beauty and the Beast.

MAN. Precisely!

WOMAN. It's the only thing she asked for.

MAN. It's not our job to keep her happy. It's our job to do what's best for the child.

WOMAN. The only thing we can give her.

MAN. Can you imagine answering the register in school? Calling for her in the playground? You can just see people's faces. 'What an unusual name. Where did it come from?' 'Well, her mother was a prostitute, you see, and she thought it might be good for business.'

WOMAN. When she said it… she meant it. I mean, she meant it in the real sense of the word. She wanted her… she wanted her to know.

MAN. She wanted *us* to know. She's *mine*.

WOMAN. We promised.

MAN. You promised.

KATYA, *their Lithuanian housekeeper, comes into the room. She is taking off her apron.*

KATYA. I say 'goodbye' now. All nice and clean and smell sweet in baby bedroom. All waiting for little princess.

WOMAN. Thank you, Katya.

KATYA. I hear pitter-patter already. I see proud Mummy and Daddy.

MAN. Not yet. We're carers until the panel decides whether her birth mother is able to –

KATYA. Believe me. You are Mummy and Daddy. She no good. She crazy lady. No home. No money. No nothing.

WOMAN. It's not quite as simple as that.

KATYA. Here you have everything. You give her everything. Give her beautiful life. She lucky, lucky baby.

WOMAN. Thank you, Katya. I'll see you in the morning.

KATYA. I get out stain from the rug. Disappeared. All gone. Katya's special magic. I give you five pound if you can find it.

WOMAN. Thank you. We'll see you tomorrow.

KATYA. And the scratch on stairs. I oil today. I oil again tomorrow. You never know it happen.

MAN. The dishwasher finished. If you could put away before you go.

KATYA. Okay.

MAN. And the blinds upstairs.

KATYA. Of course.

KATYA goes.

MAN. She arrives late and leaves early. Every day.

WOMAN. She has a long journey.

MAN. Is that my fault?

WOMAN. Let's not argue. Not tonight. This is our last night before… (*Takes his hand.*) she'll be here. This time tomorrow she'll be home. No visiting hours. No one telling us what to do. No hospital rules and dreadful tea. Just her… and us.

They hold one another for a moment.

MAN. I can feel your heart beating.

The phone rings. They let the answerphone pick it up.

VOICE. Hello. Hello. Can you pick up if you're there? Hello. Hello. We've got to close on the deal with Japan. We need a signature. We can courier the contract to you tonight. We just need to know you're there.

The WOMAN *picks up the phone.*

WOMAN. Hello.

Lights change. The baby's room on the evening of the day the baby comes home. The WOMAN *is holding the baby. The* CHILD *at her feet is playing with the bracelet. The* MAN *is standing.*

WOMAN. Must be strange. The dark. The quiet.

MAN. Us.

WOMAN. Can you believe it?

MAN. Not really.

WOMAN. I know there are explanations. Medical explanations, but it doesn't really, it's beyond explaining. Beyond us. The strangest and most extraordinary thing. Where do they come from? What are we before we know? Before we think? She's looking at me. Right into me. (*Pause.*) Hold her.

MAN. I don't want to disturb her.

WOMAN. What's the matter?

MAN. Nothing, I'm…

WOMAN. Tell me.

MAN. I'm fine.

WOMAN. You haven't held her, not properly, not long enough to feel it. To feel her.

MAN. You have to remember. We mustn't forget. She might not…

The WOMAN *puts the baby in the* MAN'*s arms. He holds the baby awkwardly.*

WOMAN. We've got to love her. She needs us to love her. Anyway, there isn't a choice. There isn't an injection against it. We're going to catch it sooner or later, so why not let it happen now?

The CHILD *reads aloud to her doll from the story book.*

CHILD. When the bad fairy had gone the room felt cold, as if it were midwinter. The music had stopped and there was no sound but the howling wind. The king ordered that every spinning wheel in the land should be destroyed and a great bonfire was built and every home searched from cellar to attic. The fire burned deep into the night and the king and queen held their baby daughter as they watched it blaze.

The baby starts to grizzle. The WOMAN *walks up and down, trying to comfort her. She is on the phone. The* CHILD *sits on the floor. The* CHILD *keeps reaching for the* WOMAN, *dragging at her legs and clothes. There is a laptop open on a chair.*

WOMAN. A black orchid at every place setting. In a specimen vase. They should have been ordered. I told them weeks ago... You'll have to go through the Yellow Pages... No white. White orchids went out the day they started selling them at the checkout in Ikea. If you can't get them, get black hyacinths, or peonies. No colour. Amaryllis if you're desperate.

The crying gets louder.

(*To the baby.*) What is it? What's the matter? Shshsh. Shshsh. (*Into phone.*) I'm going to have to go. (*To the baby.*) It's all right. (*Into phone.*) If you can't find black go very dark red. Or deep purple. Aubergine not lavender. Nothing pretty. We want sculptural. Sexy. Ring me before you decide. I'm sending the menu cover through now. Silver embossed on black.

She types an e-mail address into the laptop.

I'll speak to you later.

She puts the phone down and finishes the e-mail. The crying gets louder.

That's enough now. Quiet now. Be quiet now. Please.

She pours herself a glass of wine.

Shshshsh. What is it? What's the matter? What's the matter with you?

The crying becomes ferocious. The WOMAN *is becoming desperate.*

Stop it now. Please stop it. I don't know what you want. I don't know what to do.

ROSE *enters and takes the baby. She holds the baby on her shoulder just as she did in the hospital scene.*

ROSE. It's all right, my sweet. My angel. My beautiful. Mummy's here, my darling.

The baby starts to calm.

That's right. Mummy's here. It's all right. Everything's all right now. Everything's going to be all right.

The baby sleeps. ROSE *gives her to the* SISTER, *who walks up and down holding the baby as she speaks.*

SISTER. And of course, all Joe's friends seem to be child prodigies. We had a sleepover last weekend. The friend starts reading the newspaper at the breakfast table. 'Fiscal policy,' he reads aloud as if it were 'the cat on the mat'. 'Fiscal policy,' I hear him say as I'm pouring the Coco Pops. When his mother comes to pick up I say, 'His reading. It's amazing! Joe can hardly write his own name. Thank God we didn't call him Nathaniel like we were going to.' And she laughs and says something reassuring about 'going at their own pace', and, 'get there in the end', but I can tell. I can see she's horrified. Making mental note to discourage friendship. Then I find out later they've had a tutor. They thought he was dyslexic, apparently, because he hadn't… written his first novel. They're six years old, for Christ's sake. Oh God. Look at the time. Got to run. They're all in Pets at Home, keeping out of the rain. Daisy thinks the rabbit there's her own. Every time we go I'm terrified they'll have sold it. (*Looking at the baby.*) She's gorgeous. Completely and utterly gorgeous. Bye bye, darling. (*Kisses the baby on the head. To the* WOMAN.) Promise me you'll ring if there's anything at all. Or if there's a question.

WOMAN. Of course.

SISTER. If there's anything you want to ask.

The SISTER *hands over the baby and goes to leave. Just as she is about to exit:*

WOMAN. Do you think I can do it?

SISTER. Do what?

WOMAN. Look after her. Look after a baby.

SISTER. Of course.

WOMAN. Really?

SISTER. If I can, anyone can.

WOMAN. But you're so patient. Devoted.

SISTER. You could be. You've just had more interesting things to do.

WOMAN. Nonsense.

SISTER. It's true. It's been my life. I mean, they're my life's work. I haven't got anything else to show for it.

WOMAN. Don't say that. And, anyway, they're wonderful. What more could you want? What could be more important?

SISTER. You don't really believe that?

WOMAN. I do. It's true.

SISTER. Is it?

WOMAN. Absolutely.

SISTER. When people ask me what I 'do'. I've tried different ways of saying it. Make it sound like I've chosen, like this is my vocation, my calling. The conversation comes to a halt. You can see them trying to think of something to say next. These days people ask me about you. We saw her in the paper. We've got the book. We saw her on the telly.

WOMAN. I'm sorry.

SISTER. Don't be.

WOMAN. It must get a bit – tedious.

SISTER. No. I like it. You're my greatest achievement.

WOMAN. How can you say that? Look at them. They're amazing. You are. Amazing.

SISTER. Someone asked me when I was due yesterday. Four years it's been since I was pregnant. I try to get to the gym, but there's always something –

WOMAN. You look great.

SISTER. When you couldn't get pregnant and then the IVF didn't work, there was a part of me that was relieved. I thought, 'Thank God. There's one thing that I've achieved.' One thing that I can do that you can't.

WOMAN. Nonsense.

SISTER. But, you know, it isn't really an achievement. I mean, not something you can stand back and look at and feel proud of.

WOMAN. You should. You should feel proud.

SISTER. Should I?

WOMAN. Of course.

SISTER. There are moments. Sometimes there's a half an hour when no one's angry or mean or sulking. But it never lasts. Mostly you're just in the thick of it. Surviving. Shouting. I spend my life shouting. Then worrying I've been too strict or not strict enough. Listening to the sound of my own voice like a scratched record, saying all those dreadful things you swore you wouldn't. And you know. You know you're passing on all the worst things about yourself. Like thinking you're boring and stupid and... (*On the edge of tears*.) I'm sorry.

WOMAN. Hey. What's got into you?

SISTER. I'm sorry. It's just...

WOMAN. What?

SISTER. Since Ben started school. I know, I know I've got to
    do it. I look through the jobs section. I've even sent off for
    an application form, but what do I write when it says 'pre-
    vious experience'? There was one had a whole page for you
    to explain why you thought you were the best person for the
    job. I just stared at it. Couldn't think. Couldn't come up with
    one single reason. Can you imagine what I'd be like in an
    interview?

WOMAN. You're just out of practice. That's all.

The SISTER*'s mobile phone rings. She hands the baby back
to the* WOMAN*. She struggles to find the phone in her bag,
pulling out an array of kids' junk. She finally picks up.*

SISTER. Sorry. I'm sorry. We just got talking... What happened?

The baby starts to cry.

I'll be there in ten. They should have first aid in the shop...
    Daisy, darling. Did he bite you? Naughty rabbit. Suck it.
    Like a lollipop. (*Kisses the* WOMAN *goodbye.*) Sorry.
    Didn't mean to go on. You will ring, won't you? (*Into the
    phone, as she exits.*) You shouldn't stick your fingers through
    the bars. She thinks you're something to eat. She thinks
    you're a carrot.

Lights change. The WOMAN *paces backward and forward with
the crying baby on her shoulder. She speaks into a hands-free
phone.* KATYA *is unpacking the Ocado delivery in the back-
ground.*

WOMAN. The book says you have to maintain contact. Phys-
    ical contact. That the baby needs to know, to feel that you're
    there, no matter how long they cry. That if you put them
    down it's like a rejection. Like you're saying, 'I only love
    you when you're happy.' Like you're saying she can't
    express negative... But the other book. The book I just fin-
    ished, says you should put them in the cot after five minutes.

Then leave them to cry for five minutes and then hold them for five and leave them to cry for ten, and so on and you gradually increase the time you leave them.

The MAN *is speaking to her on the other end of the line.*

(*Continuing.*) You need to teach them, to show them that they can't. That crying won't get them… Like you're rewarding the crying if you pick them up. You're giving them the message that… You're breaking up. I can't hear you. Say that again… They need to learn. They have to realise they're not the only… I can't hear you. Ring me when you land. I said ring me from the airport. If I don't pick up we're asleep. I've got to be up at five. The car's coming for me at six. At six o'clock.

The phone has gone dead. She puts the phone down.

KATYA. When my first daughter she was baby. When she cry I put her outside in yard. I tell her, 'You come back inside when you stop crying.' And, do you know, first time she cry and cry for ever till she fall to sleep. Second time she cry for fifteen minutes. Next time for five and then after that she stop as soon as I close door.

WOMAN. But what if there was something wrong? What if she needed you? What if you weren't there and something happened? What if –

KATYA. Nothing wrong. They just want to have you wrap around their finger. (*Chucks the baby's cheek.*) Don't you, eh, darling? Yes you do, little princess. You have to show them who is boss. Who is wearing pants.

WOMAN. Trousers.

KATYA. That's right.

WOMAN. She's three months old. She's a baby.

KATYA. My daughter, she fifteen now. She good girl. She help her auntie and grandmother look after her brother and sisters. She look after her father. She write every week to her mother to say 'thank you' for the money. She grateful for everything I do for her.

WOMAN. I'm sorry.

KATYA. Why sorry?

WOMAN. I can't imagine –

KATYA. She happy. She very happy. She write me yesterday they buy television with the money I send. They use to learn English. Everybody. Whole village, they come to our house. They watch together the *Terminator 3*.

The WOMAN *picks up a carton of milk from the delivery.*

WOMAN. They've sent cow's milk. They did the same thing last week.

KATYA. I bring in the morning.

WOMAN. It's ridiculous. Why bother making an order if they're not going to send what you asked for?

KATYA. I bring tomorrow no problem.

WOMAN. That's not the point. They should send what we ordered.

KATYA. I ring them. Make complaint. Make sure they get right next time.

WOMAN. Semi-skimmed, organic goats' milk. How difficult can it be to read a list? Read a list and send what's on it, for Christ's sake.

The WOMAN *bursts into tears.*

KATYA. Is okay. I go now to Waitrose. No problem.

WOMAN. I don't understand –

KATYA. I back in half an hour.

WOMAN. I don't understand how. How can you do it?

KATYA. 'Do it'?

WOMAN. How can you leave them? How can you leave your children?

KATYA. Next Easter I go home three weeks. We speak on telephone every Sunday. Write letter. Send photo.

WOMAN. Next Easter. It's November.

KATYA. The money I send is enough to pay for my son to go to college. It pay for new roof on house. They have water now from tap. At Christmas the bonus you give me buy new shoes for everybody. They buy trainers. They send photo taken with camera I send Christmas before. Everybody. Uncle, auntie, grandmother, cousin, next-door neighbour. They all wearing trainer. Twenty-three pair of trainer. She write is best present they ever get.

The baby has fallen asleep. The WOMAN *places her in the Moses basket. Her* MOTHER *stands at the door. The* WOMAN *gestures for her to keep quiet and then tiptoes towards her, leaving the baby asleep.*

MOTHER. You're not answering the phone.

WOMAN. I've been busy.

MOTHER. You got my messages?

WOMAN. I was giving it some time.

MOTHER. How are you?

WOMAN. Fine. Fine. She cries a lot.

KATYA. I tell her. She too soft. She need to show her who is boss. She wrap around little finger.

WOMAN (*to* KATYA). You can leave this till later.

KATYA. I get milk. Semi-skimmed goat.

WOMAN. Thank you.

KATYA. You tell her listen to Katya. Katya have six children. All happy, healthy. They do as they told.

WOMAN. If you could leave us.

KATYA. Semi-skimmed goat.

WOMAN. Organic.

KATYA. Of course.

KATYA *goes*.

MOTHER. I'm sorry. I know I said all the wrong things.

WOMAN. You did.

MOTHER. It's because I care about you.

WOMAN. Let's not –

MOTHER. And I don't want you to be hurt.

WOMAN. Let's leave it. Let's try and… move on.

MOTHER. That's what I want. That's what I said in my messages.

WOMAN. I know. I heard them.

MOTHER. You should have rung. I haven't been able to sleep.

WOMAN. I needed some time.

MOTHER. When your sister said you didn't want me to see her,
I didn't know what to do. I drove round yesterday. Sat
outside for an hour. When I left the message on your answerphone, I was sitting outside. Sitting in the car. I didn't know
whether you'd let me see her. Whether you wanted me to.

WOMAN. Well, you're here now and you can see her.

They both stand over the moses basket.

What do you think?

MOTHER. She's got lots of hair. She looks… small…

WOMAN. She is… a bit… It's typical of a baby who's been
through detox.

MOTHER. Your father sends his love. Wants to come, of
course, but thought it would be better if we… first. You

know what he's like. Can't do with any disagreements.
Comes out in a rash if you talk about anything more
provocative than the weather. They sold the company, by the
way. Won't tell me how much for, but he's bought himself a
vintage Jag. Looks ridiculous, if you ask me, which of
course he didn't. Just appeared one afternoon on the gravel.

WOMAN. Isn't she lovely?

MOTHER. Of course. How are you coping?

WOMAN. Fine. Since he's been away I've been doing it on my
own, which gets a bit... exhausting.

MOTHER. Away?

WOMAN. Work. A client in Switzerland. He's back tomorrow.

MOTHER. You've been all on your own. You should have rung.
I could have helped.

WOMAN. Mum!

MOTHER. I have had two children.

WOMAN. I know. I was there.

MOTHER. Let me clear up. You sit down. Tea or coffee?

WOMAN. Coffee. Thank you. Decaf. No milk. Two sweet-
eners.

MOTHER. I know.

WOMAN. Sorry. I'm not quite...

MOTHER. You look shattered.

WOMAN. She cries a lot.

MOTHER. I heard her yesterday, from the car.

WOMAN. Last night. I thought it was never going to stop. She
sounded so distressed. As if something terrible was hap-
pening. The doctor says she's fine. I mean, he says there's
nothing wrong. Nothing to worry about. Why do they do
that? As if someone was torturing her. You feel so helpless.

Like she desperately needs something and I can't… you don't know what. Whatever you do is useless. You're useless.

MOTHER. When did she last… How often does she see her mother?

WOMAN. Birth mother. Yesterday we had contact. That's what they call it when / we…

MOTHER. Perhaps that upset her.

WOMAN. No. I don't think so. She's very good with her. Better than me… Seems to know how to… what to… I love her. I totally love her, but last night I… I was holding her and she was screaming and… I'd been awake half the night and I was so exhausted and… I screamed at her. Screamed in her face. Had to leave the room and count to a hundred.

MOTHER. You should have called me. I could have come over.

WOMAN. I didn't mean… I wasn't saying –

MOTHER. You shouldn't be alone with her.

WOMAN. What?

MOTHER. You shouldn't.

WOMAN. I'm fine. I was just exhausted.

MOTHER. It's not fair. Not right. How can you be expected…

WOMAN. What do you mean?

MOTHER. You haven't… You didn't… (*Means 'give birth to her'*.) You don't –

WOMAN. Listen. I'm not sure I'm ready for us to… I think you should come back another day.

MOTHER. Go? I only just got here. You just said you / needed –

WOMAN. I'll ring you when I'm ready…

MOTHER. You need help.

WOMAN. I'm fine, I just –

MOTHER. For her sake.

WOMAN. What?

MOTHER. You said yourself you couldn't cope.

WOMAN. I said I was tired. Exhausted.

MOTHER. Exactly.

WOMAN. What's that supposed to mean?

MOTHER. Listen. There's an agency. Angels. They provide twenty-four-hour care. They stay overnight so you can sleep. I'll pay for it. Just a couple of days a week. Then I can come in the mornings –

WOMAN. What is it? What is it about this baby?

MOTHER. What did I say?

WOMAN. Every time you open your mouth / you say something...

MOTHER. I didn't mean to criticise.

WOMAN. Implying I'm incapable. Couldn't possibly know. Like I'm a danger to her.

MOTHER. I was only saying... You've had so little experience of children.

WOMAN. I see the kids all the time.

MOTHER. Sunday lunch every couple of months.

WOMAN. Look. Let's stop now before we say / something.

MOTHER. You've had a very fortunate, very privileged existence.

WOMAN. You mean selfish.

MOTHER. That's not what I meant.

WOMAN. Selfish. Self-obsessed.

MOTHER. I didn't say that.

WOMAN. Well, perhaps I agree with you.

MOTHER. I didn't mean –

WOMAN. Perhaps that's why I want to do this –

MOTHER. You're putting words into my mouth.

WOMAN. 'Ivory tower.' That's what you said.

MOTHER. What?

WOMAN. If I live in an 'ivory tower', whose fault is it?

MOTHER. What are you talking about?

WOMAN. Who was it had me believe I had to be the best?

MOTHER. Don't you dare throw that in my face. You who had everything. Every opportunity. Whatever it took.

WOMAN. Everything but what I wanted.

MOTHER. You were the loveliest little girl. Everyone said so. Everyone.

WOMAN. Because I had to be.

MOTHER. Nonsense.

WOMAN. Because Mummy would get upset. Mummy would be disappointed. Mummy would be angry. Mummy wouldn't sleep. Mummy would drink too much and drive round and sit outside my house leaving messages on my answerphone.

The baby has started to cry.

You know, for years I believed you. I believed what you said about being special, being gifted like *you* were when you were a girl, only I would have the chance to use my talents, to do something exceptional with my life. It made me feel different from other people. Special. But, do you know. Do you know what being special really means? It means always having to prove you're better than everyone else. It means being secretly lonely and scared and never believing you're good enough but never admitting you're not, because if you're not special, if you're not exceptional, if you're frightened and anxious and insecure, who will love you? Who will want you?

MOTHER (*putting on her jacket*). All I ever wanted was to do what was best. To give you the best possible. To give you what I never.

WOMAN. I know. I know you didn't mean to.

The MOTHER *picks up her handbag and goes to the door. She is about to leave.*

MOTHER. When they're tiny, they're yours. You're the centre of their universe. You are their universe. Everything they do, they want you to see it. As if it doesn't exist until you do. Everything you say is important. Everything you do, fascinating. When I had to leave you, you'd cry, cling to me. 'Don't leave me. Please don't leave me. Don't go. Say you won't go.' I'd have to peel away your fingers. There were bruises on my arm. And then later, later when we argued, when we fought, it was because it mattered. I mattered. What I said mattered. And then, suddenly, it didn't. Suddenly I didn't. I was unwanted. An intruder. Overnight, you go from being the star of the movie to a bit part. And then an unwanted fan. A groupie. A stalker. The same child you carried inside you. The one you gave up everything for. I could have got rid of it. Girls did, you know.

WOMAN. Mother. Please.

MOTHER. She tolerates your weekly phone call. Always a reason to cut it short. Dutifully invites you for Sunday lunch once every blue moon. All of us together so you can avoid me, play the hostess, the benefactor, the lady of the manor. What's wrong with me? What's the matter with me? What have I done to make you –

WOMAN. I can't.

MOTHER. I miss you.

WOMAN. You don't. You don't know me.

MOTHER. How can you say that? I know you better than anyone. I knew you before you knew yourself.

WOMAN. That little girl. The one who didn't want you to leave.
Who left bruises on your arms. She was frightened. Frightened that she wasn't enough. Would never be good enough.
That no matter how many prizes, how many top marks, how
much praise, how pretty she looked, how beautifully dressed.
That no matter how hard she tried to keep you happy she
couldn't. How could she? She had to grow up. She had to live
her own life. She had to leave. She had to leave you.

The CHILD *talks to the doll. The* MOTHER *and the*
WOMAN *remain on stage.*

CHILD. You should be ashamed of yourself, should know
better, should be setting an example to your sister. Look at
the mess. Look at the mess you've made. That was brand
new. Don't answer back. If you do that again I'm going to
tell your father.

WOMAN (*to the* MOTHER). I'm sorry.

CHILD. Don't look at me like that, young lady.

WOMAN. I'll call you when I'm –

CHILD. What do you have to say for yourself?

WOMAN. I'll call when we're –

CHILD. Don't care? Don't care was made to care. Go to your
room and don't come out until you're ready to say –

WOMAN. Sorry. I'm sorry. I…

The MOTHER *leaves as the* CHILD *beats the doll against
the floor and then tries to destroy it in a fit of rage. The*
CHILD *hides in the doll's house, slamming the door behind
her. She reaches through the window for the doll and pulls it
into the doll's house.*

During this sequence, there is projected film of a CHILD
*running along a corridor, trying to open locked doors,
becoming gradually more frantic.*

End of Act One.

ACT TWO

The WOMAN *dreams she has lost her daughter.* REMOVAL
MEN *begin to cross the stage carrying boxes. The* WOMAN
sees the CHILD *hiding behind the doll's house. A game of hide-
and-seek in slow motion as the* CHILD *tries to flee, hiding in
the doll's house. The* REMOVAL MEN *arrive with tape and
newspaper to wrap up the house. The* CHILD *reaches through
the windows but the* WOMAN *is pushed away by the*
REMOVAL MEN *and cannot get to her. Finally they push the
doll's house across the stage. The* WOMAN *is dragged across
the stage as she clings to the* CHILD*'s hand through the doll's
house window. The* REMOVAL MEN *leave. She opens the
doll's house and it's empty. The* CHILD *has gone. Finally she
sees the* CHILD *sitting over her doll, tucking her into bed,
humming the lullaby as before. The* WOMAN *goes to her and
speaks to her.*

WOMAN. I dreamt I couldn't find you. I was dreaming I'd lost
you. I've been looking everywhere…

The CHILD *looks up. It is* ROSE. ROSE *gets up and walks
away carrying the baby.*

Lights change. The adoption centre. ROSE *is holding the baby,
completely absorbed, as the* WOMAN *looks on.*

ROSE. Hello. Hello, beautiful.

WOMAN (*to* ROSE). The cradle cap's nearly gone. We used a
new shampoo the homeopath recommended. No detergent.

ROSE. Hello. Hello.

WOMAN. She's started to smile. I wasn't sure at first. You
know how they say it can look like a smile when they've got

wind, or we call it a smile because that's what we want to see. Want to believe. We tell ourselves.

ROSE. Who's a lovely? Who's a gorgeous? Yes, yes, you are. That's right.

The baby starts to gurgle.

Mummy's precious. Mummy's sweetheart. Mummy's favourite. Aren't you? Aren't you? Yes.

WOMAN. I've written in the book, everything they said at her last check-up. That the crying, the crying doesn't mean... That it's normal for a baby that's been through what she's been... It's part of the process... So we needn't worry that it's anything more serious. There's no reason to assume that... Not yet.

ROSE. I love you. Yes, I do. Yes. Yes. Yes. Yes.

She blows a rasberry into the baby's tummy. The baby squeals. ROSE *swings her up into the air and then cradles her, smelling the soft skin of her scalp. She sings.*

Hush little baby, don't say a word,
Mama's going to buy you a mockingbird.
If that mockingbird don't sing,
Mama's going to buy you a diamond ring.

Lights change. The WOMAN, *wearing a dressing gown, sits beside the doll's house in the baby's room, wineglass in hand. The baby does not yet sleep in this room. It is late at night. The* CHILD *is sitting, combing the doll's hair. The* WOMAN *is imagining a conversation with the* CHILD *in years to come.* ROSE *is standing, as if soliciting for business on the roadside. We hear the sound of the occasional car slow down, perhaps fragments of exchanges with the punters. She chain-smokes and takes the occasional swig out of the* WOMAN'*s wine bottle.*

CHILD. Why didn't she want me?

WOMAN. She did. She wanted you very much, but she couldn't... she didn't have... she wasn't able to...

CHILD. Why did you take me?

WOMAN. Because, because she wanted you to be safe. To live with someone who could look after you properly.

CHILD. Why couldn't she look after me properly?

WOMAN. She had a very difficult life, and to make herself forget about all the bad things that had happened she would take... special medicine that made her forget all the nasty things in her life, but the special medicine made her forget all sorts of other things as well, like she might forget about you and forget to give you food and drink and –

CHILD. What sort of nasty things?

WOMAN. Her mummy and daddy, they had difficult lives too, and because they were unhappy they used to get angry and sometimes they had fights and sometimes –

CHILD. Fights?

WOMAN. They didn't mean to, but they would hurt the children. Hurt Rose.

CHILD. Hurt her? What sort of hurt her?

The WOMAN *is no longer really talking to the* CHILD, *but looking at* ROSE *who is talking to a customer, haggling over payment.*

WOMAN. They'd burn her sometimes with cigarettes and hit her in places where the bruises wouldn't show and then when she was a bit older they made her kiss and cuddle men and let them touch her so that they would give her money. And then the police took her away and put her in a special place for children who can't be at home with their mummies, but in the special place there were more bad people who wanted to do bad things.

The MAN *enters in a dressing gown and switches on the light. He doesn't see the* CHILD *or* ROSE.

MAN. What are you doing?

WOMAN. I was... looking for something.

MAN. For what?

WOMAN. I'll be up in a minute.

MAN. It's one o'clock in the morning. You were talking.

WOMAN. Was I?

MAN. It woke me up.

WOMAN. I'm sorry. I…

MAN. What are you looking for?

WOMAN. Looking?

MAN. You said you were looking for something.

WOMAN. I was wondering what we'll say. What we'll tell her.

MAN. Tell who?

WOMAN. Tell her, when she asks.

MAN. What?

WOMAN. When she wants to know. Why us? Why us, not… her.

MAN. We'll tell the truth.

WOMAN. What's that?

MAN. That Rose's unwell. That she wasn't… capable. She isn't capable…

WOMAN. How do we know?

MAN. We know.

WOMAN. Do we?

MAN. Are you serious?

WOMAN. At contact… have you noticed, Rose doesn't look at me any more. When I try to talk to her it's as if she –

MAN. Like I said, she's unwell. She's not capable.

WOMAN. Isn't she?

MAN. You've seen her case history. You know what her life's been. What her life is.

WOMAN. That doesn't mean –

MAN. Do you seriously think –

WOMAN. She's good with her. I watch her and I think, 'Why can't I be like that?'

MAN. Like what?

WOMAN. Like there's no one else. Nothing else. Like she's lost in her. Completely. Not thinking about trying to be... like I think I'm supposed to be. Like doing an act, a performance, an impersonation of a mother, whilst all the time I'm... somewhere else.

MAN. You're just getting used to it. Getting used to her.

WOMAN. I know, I –

MAN. There's a lot to take on board.

WOMAN. There is.

MAN. You're doing fine.

WOMAN. Am I?

MAN. It takes time.

He holds her.

WOMAN. Rose won't talk to me. When I talk to her it's as if she can't hear me.

MAN. You said she didn't come.

WOMAN. Before. The time before. It was as if I wasn't there. As if I didn't exist.

MAN. She's not doing herself any favours.

WOMAN. What?

MAN. It'll count against her.

WOMAN. That's not what I meant.

MAN. It'll go into the report.

WOMAN. I didn't mean –

MAN. We should make sure they tell the panel. They need to know.

WOMAN. *No.* It's not about… I *want* her to talk to me. To look at me. She won't… she doesn't… It's as if I'm… As if she… (*Struggles for the word.*) despises me.

MAN. Why do you want her to talk to you? What does it matter whether she talks to you?

WOMAN. Because…

MAN. It doesn't matter what she thinks. It's irrelevant. It's not her decision.

WOMAN. I can't get over the feeling, the thought that we're… stealing her. We're fucking up Rose's life because we want her baby. Because we want the one thing that could make her life… worth living. Make her life bearable. I feel like a criminal.

MAN. I tell you what would be criminal. It would be criminal for her to go back to a woman who fucks strangers for a living, who sleeps on the street, who's off her head with drugs or alcohol or both. Who can't get it together twice a week –

WOMAN. It's hardly a choice. She didn't choose –

MAN. It's the reality.

WOMAN. Don't you think she wouldn't rather have a different / life?

MAN. I know she had a God-awful childhood. I know it's a tragedy. I know I should feel sorry for her. Feel pity. But, do you know what? When I think of all the shit, all the toxic, poisonous crap that went into that tiny body. That tiny, defenceless body. I want to kill her.

WOMAN. When she didn't show on Wednesday I kept thinking… 'we've killed her'.

MAN. Don't be ridiculous.

WOMAN. I can't stop thinking about her… wondering what's happened. Where she… What she –

MAN. It's not our problem.

WOMAN. She wouldn't miss the session unless there was a reason.

MAN. She's an addict.

WOMAN. But she's never… She would never.

MAN. It's classic behaviour.

WOMAN. But she loves her. You can see it. She loves her more than anything. You've seen her with her.

MAN. It's not about her. It's not about us. It's about the baby. What's best for the baby.

WOMAN (*trying to remind herself*). I know. I know.

MAN. If she can't get it together to see her twice a week then what kind of mother would she make?

WOMAN. There must be a reason she didn't come.

MAN. There is. She's ill. She's a mess. That's why they took the baby away. Remember?

WOMAN. But why now? When she was doing so well. Why no phone call? Nothing. I rang them again today. Not a word.

MAN. Good.

WOMAN. What?

MAN. Good, I said. That's good.

WOMAN. What do you mean?

MAN. I mean. This is what we wanted.

WOMAN. How can you say that?

MAN. Don't you see?

WOMAN. Something terrible might have happened to her.

MAN. Look. She's left rehab. She's made no contact. If she doesn't come tomorrow. If this carries on... If this continues... she's ours. For ever. For always. Isn't that what you want? What we want?

The WOMAN *nods.*

Lights change. The WOMAN *is at home with a small* FILM CREW, *making a promotional video to accompany the launch of her book. She walks the length of the hallway as she speaks, the camera tracking backwards in front of her. The* MAN *is standing, holding the sleeping baby, elsewhere in the house.*

WOMAN. In a frantic world home should be a sanctuary, a cocoon, a place of retreat. Home is a world of our own making. A world that expresses who we are and what we believe. Home is a place of the spirit, of the imagination, where anything is possible. Here we are free to dream; to create our own reality.

DIRECTOR. Great. That's great. You look fabulous. Next section, as I said, we're going to pan round you three hundred-and-sixty-five degrees, taking in the pool, the terrace, the light well, then gradual zoom into the living room as you flop onto the Barcelona. So just walk and we'll follow. Okay? (*Beat.*) Ready?

The CAMERAPERSON *gets into position.*

Turn over and... action.

WOMAN. When you walk into your home after a long day you want to feel soothed and caressed within seconds. The stress of the day should dissolve as you hear the door close behind you.

We hear the MAN *talking to the baby as they retake.*

MAN. Daddy's here. Mummy's busy. Yes. She is. Daddy's going to give Bea her supper. That's right. Daddy's been making Bea mashed banana. Your favourite.

DIRECTOR. And... action.

WOMAN. When you walk into your home after a long day you want to feel soothed and caressed within seconds. The stress of the day should dissolve as you hear the door close behind you.

During this speech, KATYA *has entered. She is dishevelled, her coat is dirty. She has a graze on her face.*

Oh my God. What happened?

KATYA. Bloody kids.

WOMAN. Are you all right?

KATYA. Outside.

WOMAN. Sit down.

KATYA. They wait in bushes. Jump out. Jump out as I key in code to gate. They try to make me tell them number.

MAN (*carrying the baby*). We should phone the police.

He picks up the phone, starts to dial.

KATYA. I give them hell.

WOMAN. Take off your coat.

KATYA. I kick in balls.

WOMAN. Oh God.

KATYA. I scratch. I scream so loud they think I crazy.

MAN. What did they take?

KATYA. Nothing.

MAN. Nothing?

KATYA. He try, but I keep hold of bag. I bite his hand.

MAN. Katya, you should never... You should always let them take whatever. It's not worth the risk.

KATYA. Why? Why I let them take?

MAN. They could have knives.

KATYA. Why I let them win?

MAN. Or guns.

KATYA. They don't scare me. They're children. Little boys. You look into their eyes. They're frightened. They pretending to be 'big men'.

MAN (*on the phone*). A woman's just been attacked, outside our home. Just now. They wanted the code to the entrance.

KATYA (*calling*). I tell them nothing.

DIRECTOR. I'm really sorry, but the light's fading and if we don't get this now... I'm sorry. I know it's... Just this section before we lose the sunset. We need to do it now for continuity. That last take can't be used. You can hear the door opening. Her voice.

MAN. A scratch on her face. I think she's okay, just shocked. (*To* KATYA.) Is everything moving? No broken bones?

KATYA. Next time I give him broken bones. Next time I kill him. I swear.

MAN. Nothing broken.

KATYA. They think I live here. They think I rich. They try to take my necklace.

WOMAN. Oh, Katya. I'm so sorry.

KATYA. I get free with magazine. Is worthless.

DIRECTOR. So if we can go again. Just once more. And if you can look back over your right shoulder as you close the door behind you.

KATYA. They break the clasp but I keep hold.

MAN. Number 58, The Park. If you speak into the intercom we'll buzz you through the gate.

KATYA. Tell them I do identity parade. Tell them I remember the faces.

DIRECTOR. If we could have quiet now, please. Thank you. Everyone ready? Okay, turn over and... action.

Lights change. ROSE *on a street corner. Car headlights. Sounds of the city.*

A dinner party with a wealthy client at the home of the MAN *and* WOMAN. *Late evening.* ROSE *is soliciting, visible only to the* WOMAN. *She smokes.*

MAN. So, the glass arrives by snowplough. It's the latest in green technology. Converts sunlight to heat. There's been a blizzard so they can't get onto the site. It takes all day to get it off the plough. Picture, two hundred and fifty thousand pounds' worth of glass carried sheet by sheet across the snow. Finally they try to put the first piece into the frame and it doesn't fit. A millimetre too big each way. It's got to go back. All of it. I'm spitting blood. The builder swears it's the glass company. The company swears it's the builder who gave the wrong dimensions.

The GUEST *is looking at photographs of a house.*

GUEST. It looks fabulous. Stunning.

WOMAN. How much?

GUEST. What a setting.

MAN. He's bought the mountainside so no one can build near him.

WOMAN. How much did you say the glass cost?

MAN. Two hundred and fifty thousand. So, the whole lot, Thirty-two panes of it, has to go back across the snow.

WOMAN. Two hundred and fifty thousand?

MAN. Two weeks later. The glass has been recut. It fits. Thank
God. The house is looking magnificent. The client arrives.
Takes one look. 'I love it. Love it. Love everything about
it… except the glass!'

WOMAN. Two hundred and fifty thousand for the glass. How
much for the house?

MAN. 'It's too shiny!'

The GUEST *laughs.*

'Shiny?' I say.

WOMAN. How much?

MAN. 'You want glass that isn't shiny?'

GUEST. Does it exist?

MAN. Well, yes. It's twice as expensive. Has to come from
Sweden. We'll have to wait six weeks for it to arrive, which
will cost us another –

GUEST. Jesus.

MAN. 'That's what I want,' he says.

WOMAN. It's obscene.

MAN. Of course, I try to dissuade him. Spend hours trying to
change his mind. But no. 'It's too shiny.'

WOMAN. Disgusting.

MAN. It's his money. His house.

WOMAN. *We* are.

The WOMAN *fills a glass to overflowing.*

MAN (*quietly*). I think you've had enough to drink.

WOMAN. How did it happen?

MAN. More wine? (*To the* WOMAN.) Can you tell Maria we
need another bottle.

WOMAN. When did it happen?

MAN. Tea? Coffee?

WOMAN. What happened to us?

MAN. Brandy? Whiskey?

WOMAN. Brandy.

MAN (*to the* WOMAN). Can you tell Maria we're ready to clear.

WOMAN. A double brandy.

ROSE *takes the bottle and swigs.*

MAN (*to the* GUEST). What can I get you?

GUEST (*awkward*). I should be getting back. Busy day tomorrow.

WOMAN. What happened to the glass?

MAN (*to the* GUEST). Please don't feel you have to –

WOMAN. What happened to it? What did they do with it?

GUEST. Thank you for a lovely evening. Wonderful food. Delicious. You must give me her number. She's a find.

MAN. We'll speak on Monday, shall we?

WOMAN. I used to love the way you talked about buildings. About cities. As if they could change us, make us believe in something bigger, better than ourselves.

MAN. Thank you, darling.

The WOMAN *doesn't move.*

GUEST (*to the* WOMAN). How lovely to meet you.

The WOMAN *doesn't answer.*

It's been a pleasure.

MAN. Absolutely. Let me show you out.

He ushers the GUEST *to the door.* ROSE *is trying to light a cigarette. The lighter won't work.*

ROSE. Fuck. Fuck it. For fuck's sake.

The MAN *returns. He is furious but trying to control himself.*

MAN. You're drunk. I'm going to bed. You will sleep in the guestroom. When she wakes up I will feed her. Do you hear? I don't want you near her. I don't want you anywhere near her until you're sober.

She refills her glass with wine and knocks it back. He tries to take the bottle from her. She resists then swigs from the bottle.

She was a client, for Christ's sake.

WOMAN. I know.

MAN. She was here to see the house. We were about to build them one almost identical.

WOMAN. You told me.

MAN. I say 'were', because after that little performance she has probably changed her mind.

WOMAN. 'Performance'? You think that was a performance?

MAN. Look at yourself. What kind of an advertisement do you think you are?

WOMAN. Is that what I'm supposed to be?

MAN. Is it really too much to ask you to behave like a normal human being for one evening? Have you any idea how many hours, weeks, months of work have gone into this?

WOMAN. No. Tell me.

MAN. Do you know what it would mean if she pulled out? We're set to begin the foundations in two weeks. Do you realise the kind of costs we're talking about? The amount of money we'd lose?

WOMAN. No, tell me. Tell me. What does it cost to build a house like this? I mean, if you take into account everything.

The materials. The manpower. The hours of planning and
drawing and executive lunches and long-distance phone calls
and dinner parties and bottles of Krug… What if that… all
that… was used to make something… useful?

MAN. 'Useful'?

WOMAN. Something that would be of use to people.

MAN. Useful. Now there's a nebulous word.

WOMAN. Is it? Is it really? We all know what it means.

MAN. What exactly can be wrong with making something
beautiful? Inspiring. Unique. You really think it would make
the world a better place if you and I were living in some
shoebox. Because that's what you get if you want 'useful'.
Go to Russia. Go and see what kind of buildings you get if
you take away ambition, imagination, aspiration. When
there's nothing to aspire to beyond usefulness. There are
miles and miles, phalanxes, legions of identical tower blocks
as far as the eye can see. Monuments to usefulness.

WOMAN. What kind of world are we living in when two
hundred and fifty thousand pounds' worth of glass can be
thrown away whilst we allow a girl to destroy herself?

MAN. She was in rehab. She left. That was her decision. She
was given her chance.

WOMAN. Is our life really less criminal than hers?

MAN. 'Criminal'? You're telling me this is criminal? You're
telling me that if we gave all this up, it would help Rose?
You don't think that the taxes we pay, the people we employ,
the money we donate to charity, that by giving a child a
home, a future, a life, we might be more 'useful'?

WOMAN. At least she doesn't harm anyone but herself.

MAN. 'Harm'? Who do I harm?

WOMAN. Advertisement. At least she isn't pretending to be
some kind of advertisement. Some prototype for living. Poi-
soning people with some ridiculous fantasy. Some absurd

notion of life without mess. Without dirt. Without clutter. Without noise. Without... life.

MAN (*staring at her*). Are you talking about me?

WOMAN. I didn't mean...

MAN. What? You didn't mean what?

WOMAN. I'm going to bed.

She tries to leave. He restrains her.

MAN. No, don't do that. You were saying. You were telling me something.

WOMAN. I didn't say...

MAN. 'Life without... life.' Is that a reference to my sperm count? Or to your total indifference?

WOMAN. What!

MAN. You're the one who's always too tired. Too busy. Too late. Too early. Too soon. 'I've got a headache.' You actually said that last week.

WOMAN. I had a headache. People do have headaches.

MAN. Why don't you just say it? Tell the truth. Who wants to fuck a dud? A fake. A failure. What's the point?

WOMAN. It has nothing to do with you.

MAN. Then what? Then why? It's been three months since we even tried. Two years since it was worth the effort.

WOMAN. I'm sorry. I'm so sorry.

She goes to him and begins to kiss him. After a few seconds he responds, becoming passionate. Suddenly, she pushes him away. She walks away from him towards the window and the view of the city lights.

Where do you think she is?

MAN. Who?

WOMAN. What do you think she's doing?

MAN. I don't know and I don't care.

WOMAN. I look out there. (*Looking through the window.*) All those lights. Those lives. How many people are there in this city? We live so close to one another, and yet what do we know? What do we know of what goes on? The misery, the mess, the madness. We hurry home to our own little universe. Close the door. Shut it out. Hope no one comes. Wanting money. Wanting you to donate, to Amnesty or Shelter or Children in Need and finally after they've called twice and you've said you're busy and they've asked if they can call at a more convenient time and you're too embarrassed to say, 'No. No. There isn't a convenient time. There will never be a convenient time. Go away. Leave me alone. I don't want to know.' So you agree to a donation and they leave behind leaflets full of dreadful pictures and stories. Terrible stories. People drowned in a boat, trying to get to a place they could earn enough to... A whole family living under a flyover because they've lost their... couldn't afford to pay their... And a boy without a leg or a family or a home because of a war we're fighting somewhere. Rivers in China full of our rubbish, you can see the labels. Tesco. Marks and Spencer. We sell it to them to pick apart. There are whole villages that live like that, picking through our rubbish. Mountains of bottle tops, toothbrushes, ring pulls, plastic bags. Only after a while they realised the rubbish was giving off this gas. That on the way there the rubbish had started to decompose and the gas was poisonous and no one knew until they all got ill and so the government stopped them. Stopped the rubbish-sorting but then no one could eat because all the old ways had been lost since the rubbish-sorting so they left the village and went to the city where there are factories where they make our clothes and toys and washing machines and Audis. Where they work such long hours to scratch a living but still don't earn enough to... Still can't afford to... That's why they come here. Here to this city. They've seen it. Seen all the things we have. And

it's not until they get here. It's not until it's too late. I read
about a man who does three jobs and gets two hours' sleep a
night and sends every penny back home to a family he
never... He can't tell them how bad it is. How he wishes he
could go home. He wishes he never came, because he spent
their life savings to get here.

Silence.

MAN. I can't do this any more.

WOMAN. What?

MAN. This. You and me. It doesn't work. We don't work.

WOMAN. What do you mean?

MAN. I can't. I can't give you what you. I don't understand.
There's nothing I can do to mend, to fix it, to make it better.
Make it right.

WOMAN. What are you saying?

MAN. I'm so sorry.

WOMAN. Are you telling me?

MAN. I can't.

WOMAN. You're saying you want to... go?

MAN. I'm saying I can't. I cannot do it any more.

WOMAN. What about her? We'd lose her.

MAN. Her! Her! I thought we were stealing her. I thought we
were criminals. Monsters. Murderers. That's what you
said.

WOMAN. I love her.

Beat.

MAN. What about me?

Beat.

WOMAN. What?

MAN. Now that it's clear how little you respect me or what I do. What I've done for you. For us. I know that originally I was going to donate the sperm, but now it's become apparent I'm not equipped for the task, then what am I here for? To sit next to you when we go to the panel. Nod my head. Say 'Yes sir', 'No sir'. To sign my name on the dotted line. To pretend to be happy families so we can adopt a child you want to give back to her drug-addict prostitute homeless mother.

The baby starts crying. ROSE *goes to her, comforts her.*

WOMAN. I don't. I don't want. I want…

MAN. What? What do you want?

WOMAN. Us. Her.

MAN. No.

He tries to exit.

WOMAN (*suddenly*). Don't leave me. Please don't leave me. Don't go. Say you won't go. Forgive. Please forgive me. (*She clings to him.*) Those things I said. I didn't. I wasn't saying. It's not you. I didn't mean you. I love you.

The baby cries louder. He holds her.

You're shaking.

MAN. When you… When we couldn't… After you'd had all those hideous tests and they couldn't find anything wrong with you, I felt… I felt as if I'd… That no matter what I did. No matter how hard I worked or how much money I earned or how beautiful a home I made for you, I could never. I would never… But I tried to give you… I tried to make up for… to make this the most perfect home anyone had ever lived in. But then, when she came. When I saw how tiny, how helpless, how fragile. It started again. The fear, that she'd be ill, infected, damaged, broken. That they'd take her away. That there'd be nothing I could do. That I'd fail you. I'd fail you all over again.

Lights change. The WOMAN *dreams that she is holding the* CHILD's *hand. They are trying to hide from* ROSE, *taking refuge behind pieces of furniture, running between them as if in a war zone. There is the sound of a helicopter overhead and then gunfire.* ROSE *starts to fire at them with a machine gun. The* WOMAN *grabs the machine gun and beats* ROSE *to death. The* CHILD *crawls to the dead body and clings to it. The* WOMAN *drags her away.*

Lights change. Ten days later. The MAN *is waiting anxiously in the living room. It is eight o'clock in the evening. The* WOMAN *comes through the front door, carrying the sleeping baby in a car seat. The* MAN *gets up as he hears her enter.*

MAN. Where have you been?

WOMAN. I told you. The cover of the book. The reprint. They want a new image.

MAN. Your sister rang me two hours ago saying she was expecting you back at five. Your mobile's been off. She was worried sick.

WOMAN. The meeting ran on. I lost track of the time.

MAN. I rang your publisher. They said you'd left at three. It's eight o'clock. Where have you been?

Silence.

(*Shouts.*) Where the hell have you been?

WOMAN. I wasn't expecting to see her. I didn't think I'd… Didn't think she'd… She's never…

MAN. What! What are you talking about?

WOMAN. I've been there before.

MAN. Been where?

WOMAN. It's not far from the office... I walk that way from the Underground... There are lamps in the windows. Pink lamps with frilly shades like something out of a little girl's bedroom. Pink lamps under grubby curtains. Always closed. Shabby stairways winding up and out of sight. Girls standing in the doorways, or out on the street.

MAN. What did you do?

WOMAN. They're like another species, aren't they. They don't look at you, just the men. Faces painted on so you don't know. Can't see. Can't tell. You try to imagine. Try to picture what they do. What happens when they go up those stairs. What happens behind those curtains. There are all those people going to work and doing their shopping and going to look at the cover design for their new book and only feet away there's some stranger fucking a girl who's off her head because she wouldn't be able to do it if she wasn't. Did you know, I read it in the paper, ninety-five per cent of them are addicts? They need to be off their heads because no one in their right mind would do it. They need to do it to get the money to get the drugs. They need the drugs to do it to get the money to get the / drugs.

MAN. Did you see Rose?

WOMAN. I didn't recognise her.

MAN. You saw her?

WOMAN. She looked... different. Not just her clothes, it was her eyes... like she couldn't. Like she wasn't –

MAN. Jesus Christ.

WOMAN. I sat in a café across the road. She says things to men as they walk past. Sometimes they stop. Not always the ones you'd expect. A man with a briefcase and an expensive suit. An old man. Couldn't walk properly. A young boy. Just a kid. She'd disappear down a side street. Come back fifteen minutes later. It was getting dark. Then a man drew up in a car. She got into a car with a man, with a stranger, and he drove off. Can you imagine getting into a car with a / stranger?

MAN. Did she see you?

WOMAN. Can you imagine how dangerous that is?

MAN. Answer me.

WOMAN. I told you. Her eyes were… She wasn't –

MAN. Do you know what would happen if she tells them you were watching her?

WOMAN. She didn't see me.

MAN. How do you know?

WOMAN. It wasn't like it was her. It was… She was –

MAN. Can you imagine what they would say if they knew you were stalking the mother of –

WOMAN. I wasn't stalking. I wanted to know. To see –

MAN. Tomorrow, we'll ring first thing. We'll tell them you were coming back from a meeting and you saw her. Complete accident, coincidence. Say you don't think she saw you, but you can't be certain, but anyway we think they should know what she's doing.

WOMAN. No.

MAN. If she's back on the game she must be using.

WOMAN. No.

MAN. If she's using she's blown it.

WOMAN. I don't want to.

MAN. It's important information. It would be wrong to withhold it.

WOMAN. I told you. I don't want to.

MAN. It's our duty to tell. It's not about us or her. It's what's best for the child. What's best for Bea.

WOMAN. What's best for the child. What's best. Which of us knows what's best? Who's to say what damage we'll do.

What poison we have in us. What harm we're capable of. What lies we're telling ourselves.

MAN. 'Lies'? What 'lies'?

WOMAN. Everything. All of it.

MAN. Stop it.

WOMAN. It's like… like I'm living behind glass and I can't get out and no one can get in / and –

MAN. Do you want us to keep Bea?

He takes the WOMAN *by both shoulders.*

Listen to what I'm saying to you. Do you want to keep her?

The WOMAN *nods.*

Then stop behaving like a lunatic.

The baby starts to cry.

WOMAN. I wanted –

MAN. I don't pretend to understand what's going on with you, but I'm telling you, it's got to stop.

WOMAN. I didn't mean to –

MAN. When your sister rang, I could hear our daughter screaming at the other end. She was hungry. You'd left two bottles. One for lunchtime and one for four o'clock. She couldn't go to the shop because she couldn't get hold of you to tell you she was going out, and anyway she had four other kids to look after. What do you think you're doing? What the hell do you think you're doing…?

WOMAN. I'm sorry.

MAN. No more.

WOMAN. I didn't mean to leave her.

MAN. Tomorrow. You tell them what you saw. Just exactly what you saw and nothing else.

The WOMAN *nods. The* MAN *picks the baby up from the car seat.*

It's all right. Everything is going to be all right. Daddy's here. Shshsh now. Shshsh.

Lights change. The WOMAN *dreams that the* MAN *is kissing* ROSE. *They start to have sex. The sex is rough, becoming violent. He pushes her and then begins to hit her. They fight. The* WOMAN *tries to pull him off* ROSE. *There is the sound of a police siren.*

Suddenly the lights change. The sound of the police siren has changed into the sound of a burglar alarm, ringing at a deafening pitch. The MAN *is in his dressing gown. He turns on the light. The* WOMAN *is standing there alone. She has been sleepwalking. He turns off the alarm.*

Silence.

MAN. What are you doing?

WOMAN. I was –

MAN. I thought there was someone… someone in the house… I thought you were –

WOMAN. – dreaming.

MAN. – an intruder.

WOMAN. I was dreaming about you.

The baby cries.

MAN. I better go to her. You woke her up. The alarm woke her up.

The CHILD *is sitting on a chair. The* WOMAN *sits on her lap. She curls up into a ball. The* CHILD *strokes her hair.*

WOMAN. Do you remember how we used to spend all day in the river in the woods? We weren't allowed to get out. Like the land was another country that we'd never go back to.

We'd lose track of time. Forget to go home until it was dark.
All day with our feet in the water. Picking our way through
the stones and the weeds and the roots of trees. And all day
the sound. The sound of the river in our ears. Let's not go
back. Let's never go back to the house. Let's live out here.
Sleep out here under the trees. Climb up into the branches if
anyone tries to get us. Let's never go home again.

*Lights change. Evening. The sound of traffic, rain, sirens; the
city at night.* ROSE *stands at the edge of the pavement as cars
pass. She smokes. The* WOMAN *approaches slowly. As soon as*
ROSE *sees her, she tries to walk away. The* WOMAN *grabs
hold of her arm.*

WOMAN. I need to talk to you.

ROSE. I don't know you.

WOMAN. Rose.

ROSE. You don't know me.

WOMAN. Ten minutes.

ROSE. You've made a mistake.

   ROSE *walks away again but the* WOMAN *follows her.*

WOMAN. I'll make it worth your while. I'll pay you.

ROSE. What?

WOMAN. Like as if I was a… customer.

   She gets out her purse and offers ROSE *money.*

   How much is it? How much would it be to… I'll pay you
   whatever the rate. Twice the rate. Take it. Take it all.

ROSE. Fuck you.

WOMAN. I'm sorry. I didn't mean to…

ROSE. You bitch.

WOMAN. I meant…

ROSE. Coming here. Think you can pay for me. Think you can buy me.

WOMAN. I want to help you.

ROSE. Help me. You want to help me.

WOMAN. If you'll let me.

ROSE. Then fuck off. Fuck off out of my life and don't come back.

WOMAN. Rose.

ROSE. Don't call me that. Don't come here calling me that.

WOMAN. I need to understand. I need to know.

ROSE. I told you.

WOMAN. What happened?

ROSE. Are you deaf?

WOMAN. Where did you go? What happened to you? You said you were going to fight. Fight for her.

ROSE. What?

WOMAN. Beautiful, you said. The most perfect thing. Most precious thing ever, you said.

ROSE. What do you want? What the fuck do you want?

WOMAN. I want. I want you to fight.

ROSE. Are you stupid?

WOMAN. She's your child.

ROSE. Are you an idiot?

WOMAN. You love her.

ROSE. You've got what you want. You've got what you wanted. You're nothing to me.

WOMAN. You're her mother.

ROSE. You think I need you to tell me?

WOMAN. You need help.

ROSE. Fuck you.

WOMAN. There are people who can help you.

ROSE. Bitch.

WOMAN. Listen to me.

ROSE. Don't come here patronising me. Trying to make yourself feel better.

WOMAN. You can't give up. You mustn't give up.

ROSE. Can't I?

WOMAN. She's your daughter.

ROSE. Stop saying that.

WOMAN. You were doing so well.

ROSE. That's the trouble with your lot. Think anything's possible, don't you. You just have to put your mind to it. Pull yourself together. Make a choice and stick by it. Sort yourself out. Get a grip.

WOMAN. I know it's not easy.

ROSE. You don't know. You haven't a clue. You don't live my life. You know nothing. Nothing about me.

WOMAN. Why did you stop? Why did you stop speaking to me? Stop looking at me.

ROSE. Leave me alone.

WOMAN. Those things you said. That day you came to the hospital. The first time we met.

ROSE. What?

WOMAN. About her.

ROSE. Who?

WOMAN. About Beauty.

ROSE. Can't remember.

WOMAN. You can.

ROSE. Don't remember nothing.

WOMAN. You said. About her. About the animal.

ROSE. I wish she'd never been born. Wish I'd never set eyes on her.

WOMAN. Like a part of your insides. A part of you ripped out. How she could smell you. You said she could smell you.

ROSE. What you telling me for?

WOMAN. I want you to remember. You said you wanted to remember. Everything. To learn her by heart. So that when you were away from her you could still see her. Feel her.

The WOMAN *begins to open her coat. She has the baby in a sling. The baby is beginning to wake.*

Her smell. Her weight. The hair on her back. Like a monkey, you said. That's nearly gone now. Her weird little toes. They're getting longer. We had to cut her nails last week. The strawberry mark on her cheek. Look. They said it would fade, but it's still there. I hope she won't mind when she's older. It's true what you said, though. She's perfect. The most perfect thing ever. That's what you said.

ROSE. I don't want…

WOMAN. She recognises your voice. Look. She's looking at you.

ROSE. She doesn't. I don't want her to. I don't want her to remember.

WOMAN. Hold her.

ROSE. I don't want. She mustn't. I don't want her to know.

The WOMAN *suddenly puts the baby into* ROSE*'s arms.*
ROSE *stands holding the baby. She can hardly bear to look
at her. Moments pass.*

Tell her. Tell her that I loved her but I can't. I couldn't…
couldn't take care of her. Tell her… Tell her I gave her to
you to look after.

WOMAN. To me?

ROSE *nods.*

Why me?

ROSE. Because… you can.

WOMAN. But it's not right.

ROSE. No.

WOMAN. It's not fair.

ROSE. I know.

WOMAN. It shouldn't be.

ROSE. No.

WOMAN. I don't understand… Tell me. Why did you stop
coming? What happened? What happened to you?

ROSE. …I was starting to feel…

WOMAN. That's good.

ROSE. No. It isn't. It's bad. I'm full of bad.

WOMAN. You're not.

ROSE. You don't know. You don't know me.

WOMAN. I saw you with her. Saw how you were with her.
What you could give her.

ROSE. 'Give her'?

She extends her arms to give the baby to the WOMAN. *The*
WOMAN *doesn't move.*

That's what I can give her. I can save her. Save her from me. Like I wanted to be saved. Goodbye, my beautiful. My sweet. My darling.

WOMAN. I can't. I can't take her.

ROSE *tries to push the baby back into the* WOMAN*'s arms. The* WOMAN *shakes her head, refusing to take her.* ROSE *kisses the baby on the head and puts her down gently on the pavement. She walks away into the night.*

Sound of traffic, sirens, rain. Headlights pass.

The baby starts to cry.

The End.

A Nick Hern Book

Mine first published in Great Britain as a paperback original in 2008 by Nick Hern Books Limited, 14 Larden Road, London W3 7ST, in association with Shared Experience

Mine copyright © 2008 Polly Teale

Polly Teale has asserted her right to be identified as the author of this work

Cover image: Eureka! (www.eureka.co.uk)
Cover design: Ned Hoste, 2H

Typeset by Nick Hern Books, London
Printed and bound in Great Britain by CPI Antony Rowe, Chippenham, Wiltshire

A CIP catalogue record for this book is available from the British Library

ISBN 978 1 84842 004 5

FSC
Mixed Sources
Product group from well-managed
forests and other controlled sources
Cert no. SGS-COC-2953
www.fsc.org
© 1996 Forest Stewardship Council